How to
RIG AND FISH
NATURAL
BAITS

How to
RIG AND FISH
NATURAL
BAITS

Byron W. Dalrymple

Drawings by
Charles Dougherty

OUTDOOR LIFE ● FUNK & WAGNALLS
New York

Times Mirror Magazines, Inc.
Book Division

Editor and Publisher	John W. Sill
Executive Editor	Henry Gross
Associate Editor	Neil Soderstrom
Art Director	Jeff Fitschen
Production Manager	Millicent La Roque
Editorial Assistants	Pat Blair
	Ellen Patrisso

Library of Congress Catalog Card Number: 76:014670
Funk & Wagnalls Hardcover Edition: ISBN 0-308-10289-4
Paperback Edition: ISBN 0-308-10291-6

Small portions of the section on freshwater fishing in this book are excerpted from or based upon an article by the author that appeared in Fawcett's FISHING JOURNAL, *Copyright 1976 by Fawcett Publications, Inc.*

Manufactured in the United States of America

To Pete Barrett,

who sparked the idea
for this book.

Contents

INTRODUCTION — **Bait Fishermen Versus Purists** 1

PART **1 — Equipment for Bait Fishing** 6
  Hooks 8
  Sinkers 17
  Floats 24
  Snaps and Swivels 28
  Leaders 29
  Spinners 29

PART **2 — Rigs for Bait Fishing** 32
  Freshwater Rigs 33
  Saltwater Rigs 47

PART **3 — Freshwater Baits and How to Fish Them** 58
  Minnows 60
  Suckers for Muskies 71
  Cut Bait 74
  Worms and Night Crawlers 77
  Frogs 83
  Crayfish 86
  Grasshoppers and Crickets 90
  Grubs and Caterpillars 94
  Hellgrammites and Other Nymphs 95
  Salamanders 97
  Salmon Eggs and Roe 101
  Other Baits 103

PART 4—**Saltwater Baits and How to Fish Them**   107
Saltwater Baitfish   112
Menhaden   114
Mullet   114
Killifish   115
Anchovy   115
Sardine   116
Silversides   117
Flying Fish   117
Needlefish   117
Mackerel   118
Ribbonfish   118
Other Species   119
Chumming   123
Chunk Baits   126
Strip Baits   128
Eels   135
Crustaceans   138
Mollusks   149
Marine Worms   155
Squid   153

Index   161

How to
RIG AND FISH
NATURAL
BAITS

Bait Fishermen Versus Purists

ONE OF THE most amusing incidents I can ever recall of a confrontation between a bait fisherman and what I would call a purist occurred one summer on a river in western Montana. I was not a participant, only an observer.

In summer certain Montana rivers get an upstream movement of outsize Dolly Varden trout. They spawn in headwater tributaries in fall, but the movement up to those sites may start far down as early as June. Supposedly the fish do not eat during this long run, but this is probably one of those partial truths. For whatever reason, they whack a lure now and then and on occasion also take solid nourishment.

In Montana the handsome Dolly Varden is called a "bull" trout. Quite a few natives living along the run streams are avid bull-trout fishermen. Dolly Vardens are not very discriminating in their tastes, and among those who use bait, one really preposterous item is a favorite—a whole leg of a ground squirrel, locally known as a "gopher," skewered on a big hook and let back below a log jam or some other likely hiding place in a deep hole.

I had been fly fishing a nearby small stream for cutthroats and had paused beside this big Dolly Varden river to eat a tailgate lunch. Close to me a classic native "country fisherman" dressed a bit like an old-time lumberjack from the 1890s was working away, intent on slipping some sort of terminal inducement at the business end of stout, beat-up, and ancient tackle into the jackstraw interior of a debris-filled hole. He chewed tobacco and spit copious squirts at intervals into the roiling river. I appraised him as one who knew these parts and who was no stranger to large-bore bull trout on his table. He said nothing, so I kept my silence, too.

Presently from upstream a rather dapper angler appeared. He carried a fly rod, and I guessed he had been shooting large streamers into the holes to try to inveigle a big Dolly. It often works. Certainly nothing wrong with that. I've done it, too, and successfully. Further, to each his own. But he destroyed whatever rapport he might have had when, as the native hauled in his line and examined his bait, the interloper arched his brows and said in an obviously nonnative voice and accent: "What in the name of heaven is *that?*"

The bull-trout man spat a fine arc of brown juice. Without looking at his questioner he replied, "Gopher leg."

The other recoiled as if struck in the face with it. "For a *trout?*" He was incredulous.

"That's how I figure." Then the native, who was actually rather guileless since he already knew who he was and why, added the perennial question: "Caught anything?" Or *was* he guileless?

Disarmed, the outstater said, "Well, frankly, no." Then, almost in apology: "How about you?"

Now the other dropped the bomb. "Not much," he said. "Just a couple. Them two." He leaned down and raised a stringer tied to a bush. It seemed to me three minutes were required to get the entire length of the trout out of the water. I'd guess they weighed 12 pounds each. That was the end of the confrontation.

Now I don't even intend this book to include such items as gopher legs as "bait." That's way outside our province. I use the incident to illustrate the fact that quite a large number of freshwater fishermen look down their noses at those who use bait. These anglers, mesmerized by artificial lures, choose to believe that bait fishing really isn't much of an art, and some claim it's not even a sporting method. They believe, no doubt sincerely, that artificial lures are far and away more productive. A few even envision bait fishermen as old-fashioned, corny characters in bib overalls, maybe not very bright. But all too often the artificials enthusiasts shoot their best arguments full of holes by complaining that the bait crowd decimates the fish populations!

For some odd and never clearly explained reason, the saltwater scene is not the same. To be sure, artificial lures are used extensively and successfully in saltwater. Plugs, spoons, jigs, and even flies catch numerous marine species. But the influence of artificials has been by no means as extensive among saltwater fishermen as among freshwater anglers. On the coasts bait and artificial-lure anglers fish happily side by side, and indeed a great many marine enthusiasts regularly interchange natural bait and lures, using whichever is more productive at the moment. By and large, however, probably far more than half of all saltwater anglers never use anything but bait. Quite a number of saltwater species are difficult or practically impossible to attract with artificials. Indeed, to this day natural bait remains the standard of marine fishing.

All of the arguments against bait fishing, fresh or salt, are ridiculous anyway. Antibait purists are a little like antihunters. The latter have never hunted, and don't intend to, which would be fine, except that because they dislike hunting they insist that those who do enjoy it should cease. I have no quarrel whatever with the purist artificials fishermen, as long as they do not try to force me to think as they do. Some seasons I fish lures almost entirely. But whenever I feel like bait fishing or believe it will help me catch fish, I switch, and I've never had any guilt feelings about it.

It is true that even in ancient times fishermen experimented with artificial lures. For example, there is authentic evidence that such rigs as a thorn hook with a small seashell spoon twirling rather awkwardly ahead of it on a plant-fiber line were used and presumably caught fish. The basic idea, however, was not to be more "sporting" but simply to catch food in a pinch when no bait was available. Izaak Walton evidently was wholly a bait fisherman, yet he is considered the father of modern sport angling. Who could seriously contend, from Walton's writings, that he knew no art in angling?

Certainly there is immense enjoyment in casting artificial lures and catching fish on them. Yet this should not mean that there should be any stigma attached to fishing with bait. The expert bait fisherman indeed practices an art, as witness the fact that some bait anglers mop up and some don't, just like the users of artificials. A friend of mine who uses both likes to remind uppity lure fishermen that all they're doing is using a fake bait!

In early 1975 I was assigned by *Outdoor Life* magazine to do a story about the enjoyment, the art, and the productiveness of fishing with a cane pole, bobber, and bait for bass and panfish. The research for that story took me back to boyhood. I have long claimed that bobber and bait fishing is one of the most dramatic of angling sports. Many a youngster started that way. Then, as it is said, he "graduated" to casting with artificials. Nonsense! He didn't graduate. He gave up an infinitely dramatic endeavor for one really seldom half as much so.

Part of the time while renewing my acquaintance with the cane pole, I fished on a lake that I built on property of ours. I suddenly realized all over again, and fully, what it meant to move a boat *quietly*. With a cane pole you have to get *close*. I learned all over again how to be quiet myself, in the boat. And how to reach gingerly out to flip a baited hook into a small pocket without disturbing the fish. Modern big-boat, big-motor anglers have never learned such arts. They zoom and carom, cast a country mile. As a cane-poler I was put suddenly, by the restrictions of my tackle, on intimate terms with my quarry. But the real drama was brought back to me as I watched the bobber. Of course, you can fish an artificial fly down below a bobber. If you move it by crawling the bobber along, you may catch something. But try leaving it still and it is a total dud. A fish may nose up to it, then turn aside. A worm — any bait — however is something different.

Any fish knows that it is good to eat, undoubtedly partly from past experience, but probably mostly from smell. It also looks edible, and when nibbled it feels right. If fish do have a developed sense of taste, which they may, it tastes right. So a bait without any question has several advantages that artificials lack. Regardless of propaganda to the contrary, if fish won't take bait it's likely they won't take artificials either. *But* time and again when fish won't strike artificials, they'll eagerly seize a bait. So it's awfully hard to argue cogently in favor of artificials. You either want to catch fish or you don't.

Recently, in fact, again on my own lake, I watched from the cover of a tree shadow by the dam as a bass of possibly 4 pounds cruised slowly nearby. Eagerly I pitched a lure out past the fish and worked it near. The bass spurned it. I tried several different kinds. The brute would not even look. So, the heck with him. I rigged with a worm-baited hook and a bobber and tossed out to catch a redear sunfish if I could. Shortly I had one. As it protested on the way in, that big bass literally exploded out of the weeds and belted it. He didn't get it, and I didn't get him, but he certainly knew what was good to eat—in his then selective mood—and what wasn't.

While I researched that cane-pole story, I was reminded again of the beautiful anguish of watching a dancing bobber with bait below. It lies first inert upon a flat surface. Then suddenly it jiggles. You tense. You snug line, oh so gently. The bobber skitters aside, goes under. You start to set the hook, but it pops up again. None of this would happen if an artificial dangled below. Further, when you cast an artificial lure and wind it in, there is a strike, and you grind away. The strike is a split-second thrill. Bait fishing with a bobber drags the exquisite excitement out almost unbearably. Suddenly down the bobber goes. You haul back. Of course this is an art! Of course it is sporting!

Or consider the saltwater fisherman drifting in a small boat on a quiet bay along the Gulf of Mexico. He knows that schools of spotted weakfish— or, as most fishermen call them, "speckled trout"—are feeding here over grass flats, hunting shrimp. He can see the swirls they make and now and then hear the *slosh* as one smacks a shrimp right at surface.

He is fishing with what any inshore marine angler would instantly recognize as a "popping cork rig." The bobber is weighted and has a dish-faced top. Down below it 1 or 2 feet is a live shrimp on a hook. When the angler jerks with a quick, short motion the cork makes a pop, and a sloshing surface swirl. Simultaneously, the shrimp dances upward and falls back. Sound and sight both attract predaceous trout.

Whammo! A big trout slams the dancing shrimp. Down goes the popping cork. But no—up it comes again. Then down once more, and this time the angler is quick enough to set the hook. There is no finer fishing drama than this, nor one to make adrenalin flow faster. Who would say it is neither sport, nor sporting?

There are also scores of instances when bait fishing solves a problem with which artificials do not seem able to contend. Some years ago when I lived in northern Michigan, in a period long before fishing with artificials for big spring-run rainbow trout had become refined enough to produce much there, a group of fishermen devised a successful manner of fishing a night crawler. In order to catch fish, it had to be on bottom in the swift Sturgeon

River near which I lived. And it had to wash and curl and tumble naturally. Fished with a hunk of lead and a tight line, no 5-pound trout would touch it.

So, these schemers used fly rods, and they replaced the fly line with heavy monofil. A short-shanked, sturdy hook was tied to line's end and baited with a big night crawler. Over the first 6 or 8 feet of the line a split shot was pinched on about every 6 inches. The line was then fed carefully into a rush of water above a big hole. This rather awkward rig was in its time a bombshell invention. The shot laid the length of line on bottom, and it curled around in the deep-hole current. The bait, unweighted at the end, tumbled and waved but was kept on or very near bottom.

The rig was pure murder. While purists cast their arms loose and only caught a small trout here and there in the roily spring water, the guys with those jumbled-up bait rigs that really didn't look, I'll admit, very artistic or sporty, had big trout jumping all over the river. The very awkward attributes of this setup made fishing it a real art. And as far as sport was concerned, catching several busters that way certainly beat catching nothing!

So, if you happen to be in an area where there are those who frown upon the use of bait, don't let it bother you. It is as much fun and just as much of an art as hurling a hunk of metal or a puff of feathers. I am an avid fly fisherman, and I also dearly love to fish surface plugs for bass. But I started out as a kid fishing bait, and I've never given it up completely and never intend to. One reason is that I like to catch fish, and bait will often accomplish this when artificials fail.

PART 1

Equipment for Bait Fishing

TO ALL FISHERMEN who were initiated as children, the nostalgic remembrances of those first experiences are invariably the brightest. My first recollections date back to when I was five years old and went along, chiefly as an observer, with my father. Oddly, my father was not a fisherman at all. But we lived in a small farmhouse only a short walk from the bank of the Flint River in the Thumb area of southern Michigan, and fishing periodically was not so much a matter of sport—but rather a form of gathering food.

We were quite poor people. I chuckle often nowadays, thinking of my boyhood and imagining what the federal and state governments would have been doing had they been geared then as they are today. Case workers would have been swarming over us. We had no electricity, no refrigeration, no indoor toilet. My mother cooked on a wood stove, we pumped water from a well and slept on homemade mattresses stuffed with corn husks or poultry feathers from chickens, ducks, and geese we had eaten.

We used gobs of cholesterol-heavy home-churned butter, drank unpasteurized milk straight from the cow, ate home-raised fresh and canned vegetables, fruits and meat, and fish from the Flint and a swampy pond near it. My father made $25 a month teaching country school. Obviously we were disadvantaged, sad health-hazard cases. But there were no government planners then to explain all that to us, and so we were happy, and physically tough as tripe. Some of the happiest moments, for me at least, were those spent trudging barefoot down the dirt road to the Flint, feet plopping in the thick dust churned fine by passing wagons and horses and buggies.

My father carried the long cane pole and the rusty tobacco tin with the fresh-dug worms in it. Usually he went to the pond, which was alive with bullheads. The impetus for this fishing expedition arose when the earthen bullhead crock in the cool dirt root cellar under the house became empty.

My paternal grandmother, who lived with us, had a way of skinning bullheads and peeling the skeleton out, so that a double fillet could be laid flat. These were placed in salt in the big crock—a layer of salt and a layer of bullheads alternately. They would keep thus for several weeks, but they seldom got the chance. They tasted too good shaken in flour and fried in butter!

I describe in detail the setting in this preauto period early in the present century, the better to set the stage for introducing the tackle that was customary, with us and with our country neighbors along the river. Hooks were few, nondescript, of assorted shapes and sizes. There were no preferences. You had what you had. One was exceedingly careful not to lose hooks. Some of ours had been passed down from the previous generation.

There was a small wooden salt-codfish box in the woodshed into which odds and ends of bolts, nuts, and once-used nails were always dropped to await a time when one was needed. From this box came the sinker supply. A small stove-bolt nut was favored. The stout braided salt-and-pepper fishing line was simply run through the center and tied in a hard knot, placing the sinker several inches above the hook.

I vividly remember that our two bobbers, or floats, fascinated me. Whittling was a pastime of all country people in those days, and an uncle who often visited us loved both to fish and to whittle, and so he had fashioned these floats, smoothed them nicely and painted them with red barn paint. They were very light, probably of cedar. Each end tapered from an oval center and had a notch cut in it. The line was twisted into a loop in both notches and pulled snug.

With high anticipation I'd watch my father bait the hook, reach out the long pole and drop the rig with a minor plop into the black water of the "bullhead hole," as the pond was known. Soon the red bobber would dance, finally duck under, and my father would haul up a shiny, struggling, flopping bullhead. They were as black as the water, but some had a bright yellow belly. Taking them off the hook without getting stung by the sharp fin spines was a high art.

After my father had caught several he'd always ask if I'd like to hold the pole. He had a little joke of asking as if he was sure I didn't want to, when of course I couldn't wait. At first I needed help, but later on I fished with a pole of my own, and on the bank of the Flint. The procedure was to cut a forked willow, thrust the sharpened stalk into the soft earth near the water and lay the pole in the crotch. A bare foot placed on the butt of the pole held it while eyes were glued to the bobber.

There is something about the remembrances of the rudimentary equipment we used that to me illustrates as nothing else could the simple joys and excitements of bait fishing. I can recall when somehow those hand-whittled bobbers had disappeared and my brother and I would make do with a short piece of pithy elderberry branch cut from a streamside bush. Whether or not the pleasures of that early fishing were greater than those of today is academic. We used such equipment because it was all we had, and very little was obtainable anyway.

Certainly today's equipment is greatly changed, far more efficient and varied. There are hooks, sinkers, floats, leaders designed for every imaginable situation and fitted, many of them, to individual species of fish. Bait fishing, along with fishing with artificials, has grown mightily in sophistication and specialization.

Hooks

The fishhook is one of man's oldest tools, dating back thousands of years in varied forms. It is interesting that only over a comparatively brief period have hooks been designed for any use except bait fishing. The original "hook" is thought to have been the gorge, a piece of stone, bone, or shell pointed on each end and with a groove in the middle to which a line, probably of fiber or sinew, was tied. Bait was thrust upon one end, or perhaps both. A fish presumably swallowed the gorge lengthwise, but a yank on the line turned it crosswise, and the fish could not disgorge it.

Later, during the New Stone Age, actual hooks carved from bone or antler appeared. Then about 5000 B.C. metals came into use, and copper fishhooks were fashioned. Progressively they grew more refined, and in modern times extremely so and infinitely varied. Today there are hundreds of hook sizes and designs. But only a few basic types need concern the bait fisherman.

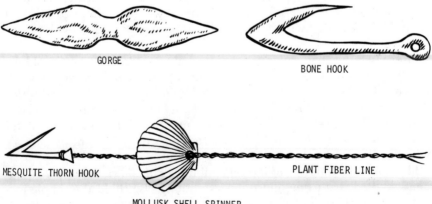

The gorge was a hooking device used by primitive man. During the New Stone Age, hooks carved from bone or antler were used to catch fish. The thorn hook and shell spinner were used by early American Indians.

The type of hook you use obviously must be selected according to the species of fish and its physical attributes and the tackle you will use. A hard-mouthed species, for example, will require a point that can be rammed home easily. A soft-mouthed variety requires a hook that won't tear flesh too severely. Fish with small mouths need to be fished for with small hooks, those with large mouths need a hook with a big, deep bite. However, an angler using light, flexible spinning tackle may not be able to send home a hook of heavy wire, yet one of light wire will be sensitive to his strike.

There are other extremely important considerations: the type of bait to be used; the hook design that will hold it best, damage it the least, and allow it, if alive, to stay so the longest; whether the water is cluttered with debris or open; whether you will be fishing in fresh- or saltwater.

There are several hook finishes, and each has its enthusiasts. For example, many hooks for freshwater are available in a gold finish. I happen to believe that the shiny gold hook has a high fish appeal. I know many bait fishermen who agree. For some purposes, such as crappie fishing with small minnows, they use nothing but gold. Maybe this is just whimsy. Anyway, gold finishes are available.

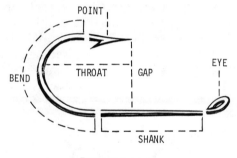

Parts of a hook.

The old standard blued finish is still popular, and cheap. This is a finish for freshwater work. Bronzed finishes also are popular. Bronze is corrosion resistant in freshwater but not in salt. Hooks made from an alloy of nickel and steel are expensive but do not corrode in saltwater. Stainless-steel hooks hold up fairly well in saltwater also. Tin plating is used on many saltwater hooks, and presently one of the best and most popular platings for use in corrosive waters is cadmium.

The following are some of the most popular and efficient hook designs for bait fishing, with brief remarks about their advantages and faults. Bear in mind that, as with all fishing equipment, each design is a compromise of sorts. The thing to do is to experiment broadly and then select hook types most suitable to the kind of fishing you most avidly pursue.

Aberdeen. For panfish and other freshwater fish in brushy waters the Aberdeen is an excellent choice. It is made of tempered light wire so it will bend before breaking. Thus when hung up you can pull it loose and reshape the bend. The Aberdeen bend is round and wide. "Wide" refers to the distance between point and shank. Wide bends are very good for minnow fishing. The point extends far enough to prevent it from reembedding itself in the bait. The Aberdeen style also has a long shank. This makes removal easy. Long-shanked hooks of any design are also most suitable when fishing for species with teeth. The hook length keeps fish teeth away from the line or leader.

Carlisle. This is another design with a round bend and an extra-long shank popular with minnow and night-crawler fishermen. The shank length helps keep the quarry from swallowing the hook. The point, while straight, is slightly offset. Offset points are of several types. The term means that the line from barb to tip, or from farther down in the bend of the hook, is at an angle to the line of the shank. Many users claim that offset designs give better hooking qualities and are harder for a fish to "throw" because the point is likely to bite flesh, on a leap for example, rather than slip free.

Kirby. Offset points are often said to be "kirbyed," after the design of this popular style. Other hook styles termed "reversed" are simply those in which the offset is in the opposite direction from that of the Kirby. The Kirby standard ordinarily has a shorter shank than the Carlisle. It has long been a popular bait-fishing hook. However, there are some disadvantages to all offset points and bends. One is that in some instances, when using minnows for instance, the offset point gouges back into the bait. Another is

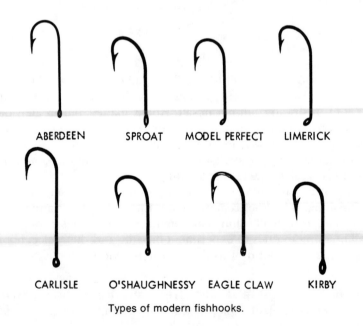

ABERDEEN   SPROAT   MODEL PERFECT   LIMERICK

CARLISLE   O'SHAUGHNESSY   EAGLE CLAW   KIRBY

Types of modern fishhooks.

that when trolled or retrieved by reeling, a baited offset design tends to revolve or spiral and twist.

Sproat. This bend is slightly narrower in gap and is parabolic rather than round. It is a very old design suited to freshwater fishing, has a straight point and is very strong. The Sproat might be termed a kind of all-purpose freshwater bait-fishing hook.

O'Shaughnessy. This is probably the most popular hook for general use in saltwater. It is usually made from heavy material and is exceedingly strong. Slow-biting fish and those with large, heavy mouths are solidly hooked by it. One of the reasons is that the point is designed with a slight outward slant. This presumably makes hooking a fish somewhat surer. This hook is renowned among freshwater trotliners as well as saltwater anglers. The bend is fairly similar to that of the Sproat.

Limerick. This is a very sturdy type of hook with a straight point and a half-round bend. It is one of the most popular of all fishhooks.

Model Perfect. This is a design anyone can use "when in doubt." The bend is round, the gap is wide, and the wire from which it is made is light. We should note here that round-bend, light-wire hooks put only a very small hole in the flesh of the fish. This has its advantages while the fight is on. The other side of the coin is that in a soft-mouthed species the light wire may cut and make the entry hole larger, and the round bend, especially with a straight point, may slip out more easily.

Eagle Claw. Everyone knows this brand name. The hook styles for Eagle Claw are, however, truly an American design. The firm manufactures hundreds of styles, including most of the designs already described. But the basic feature of the Eagle Claw is that the pull of the line is direct, from hook eye to point, because the point curves inward on a line with the eye.

There are scores of specialized designs other than those just described. Wide-gap bends are available and offer extra hooking space. Several styles for tuna fishing and similar ones used on the Texas coast for deep fishing for red snapper have a bend that is almost a circle. The point continues the circle, curving far inward. Most of these have offset points. This style holds the bait well and keeps the fish on while it is retrieved from deep water. The Siwash salmon hook, born in the Pacific Northwest, has a relatively short shank, a wide gap and deep bite — depth of throat — and a long spear-type point. This style holds large baits well and drives home very efficiently.

I'm sure all anglers are familiar with weedless hooks. Most utilize a long, thin loop of springy light wire, fastened to the shank near the eye and with a bent-down opening at the bottom of the loop that catches below the point. This allows most weeds to slide past and yet offers little resistance to a strik-

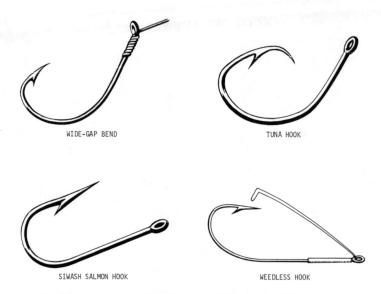

WIDE-GAP BEND

TUNA HOOK

SIWASH SALMON HOOK

WEEDLESS HOOK

Among specialized hooks, wide-gap bends are available that provide extra hooking space. Tuna hooks and some others have almost a circle bend. The Siwash salmon hook has wide gap and deep bite. The weedless hook prevents hangups in overgrown waters.

ing fish. Some weedless designs employ a light rubber band, slipped through and hooked over the eye, then stretched to hook under the barb. These also work efficiently.

Several hook styles are exaggerated designs that look as if they would have trouble hooking anything, yet these have their enthusiasts. One that some anglers, especially ice fishermen, swear by is the Kahle Horizontal. This in a rather similar bend is also sometimes called an English bait hook. It has an extra-wide bend. Enthusiasts of the style claim it has excellent deep-hooking ability. A further far-out exaggeration is a model favored by some ice fishermen for pike, and usually called a "pike hook." This one almost forms a triangle. The shank comes down on a slant, the "bend" is a straight horizontal line, the point slants up and inward. It is difficult to imagine any advantage in this design, but again, some winter pike fishermen swear by it.

Several hook styles tailored particularly to minnow fishing but useful for some other baits, too, should not be overlooked. Among these are the "double" bait hooks, usually either two hooks coming from a single shank, or else two with their own shanks brazed together and with a single eye. Some of these have a sharp U-shaped pin linked into the eye as a second

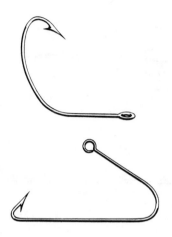

Top: The Kahle horizontal hook.
Below: The pike hook used for
ice fishing.

place for impaling the bait, to keep it straight. Some single hooks have the same device. Other doubles are full rigs made up with beads and spinner and mono-leader plus swivel to which the line is attached.

Among the most intriguing of the doubles are the so-called "safety-pin" hooks for minnow fishing. A steel pin and catch are attached to one side. This is run through the minnow from the vent and out the mouth, where it is snapped into the clip. On some the double hooks ride with bends and points up, along the rear sides of the minnow. Others, undoubtedly more effective, ride with hooks down, which means pin and catch are on the outside, behind the hooks.

A few years ago I was fishing for lake trout in the spring in northern Ontario. The guide wanted to troll, and he used a hook rig for large sucker minnows that I've never seen elsewhere, and I'm not sure that it is available

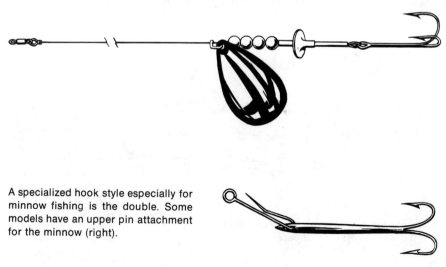

A specialized hook style especially for
minnow fishing is the double. Some
models have an upper pin attachment
for the minnow (right).

13

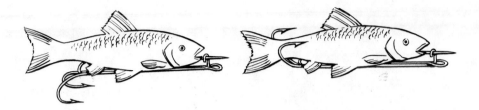

Safety-pin double hooks for minnow fishing.

in stores. It was a big pin-type hook similar to the doubles described above, except that there were three treble gangs arranged along it. The pin was run through the big bait, and a single hook from each of the first two trebles was embedded in the back. The third treble overrode the tail.

A device rather similar and possibly more effective was used years ago in New York State for lake-trout trolling. I corresponded for some years with Fred Streever, the gentleman who conceived the design. It also used three treble gangs, but they were tied along a line, spaced possibly an inch apart. Ahead of them a small hook was tied in, which was used to hook a big min-now through both lips. A short piece of fishline then bound the baitfish behind the gills to the line. Then a hook of each of the first two trebles was thrust into the back of the bait. As I recall, the second treble was secured with the bait a bit curved. This insured that it would spin when retrieved.

Whether the above should be placed here under "hooks," or later with "rigs" or "minnow fishing," may be debatable. But basically these are hooks,

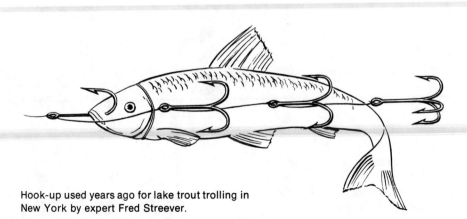

Hook-up used years ago for lake trout trolling in
New York by expert Fred Streever.

and it is almost impossible to describe the devices without telling how the bait is arranged. Another in the same category is the so-called "frog harness." I have not seen any of these used for a long time, possibly because frogs are not as much used nowadays for bait as they once were. However, the frog harness hook setup is still available here and there and has a few enthusiasts.

There have been many types. One I noticed recently in Herter's (Waseca, Minn.) big mail-order catalog is designed so that it won't kill the frog. In fact, it allows the frog to kick its legs normally. There is a large, long-shanked hook with a ring brazed to it. The back legs and rear part of the frog's body are slipped back through this ring. A small hook brazed to the

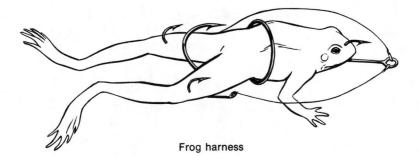

Frog harness

hook eye secures the frog through both lips. The large hook rides with bend and point up, at the crotch. Two small hooks on lengths of limp nylon are attached to the hook eye, brought rearward and hooked lightly into the outer thigh portion of each back leg.

Treble hooks certainly are not to be overlooked by bait fishermen. For example, saltwater speckled-trout (spotted-weakfish) anglers on the Texas coast taught me long ago to use them when fishing live shrimp. The mouth of a trout is soft, and the treble holds it better than a single hook. There is a specialized treble I want to mention that has found great popularity with

Treble hooks should not be overlooked by bait fishermen. Special treble with coil used to hold cheese (right) works well with natural bait such as mollusk meat.

Hooks for salmon eggs are very short-shanked, work well also with small grubs.

those who use cheese, marshmallows, dough baits, etc. It has a brass spring coil running round and down the shank. I've discovered these work quite well with certain soft natural baits, such as mussels.

Hooks for salmon-egg fishing are very short-shanked. The basic design and use will be covered later under salmon-egg fishing. Some of these small, short hooks are excellent also for use with grubs and other small natural baits. They can be entirely buried in the bait. The Eagle Claw Bait Holder hooks have barbs cut into the outside of the shank. These point out

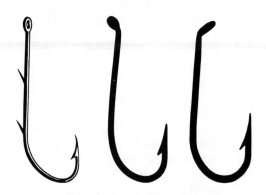

The Eagle Claw Bait Holder hook. It has shank with barbs made by slicing into edge of shank. These help hold bait in place.

Up-eye and down-eye hooks.

and up, to hold a worm or other bait and keep it from bunching up on the bend. Some bait fishermen favor a hook with a "down eye," which is an eye that's bent inward, giving a more direct line of pull on a plane with the point. There are others who like the "up eye," which means the eye is bent outward. The pull presumably rams the hook deep and keeps a deep bite during the battle.

Most of the hook styles noted can be had in standard shank, long, short, and extra-long. Likewise most are available in fine, light wire, and heavier wire. Bear in mind that a light hook allows freer action of a live bait. Various point styles also are available. Straight points are in a plane parallel to the shank. These may have a hollow (curved) inner surface or be a straight spear. These points set easily, hold well, but need sharpening often for they dull or blunt easily. Many saltwater bait hooks have a "rolled"

Types of hook points.

point. This means the point is bent in toward the shank. A variation is the bent-in point. On this one the entire spear is bent inward. Extremes of this are the circle bends mentioned previously. The gap is not large, but the hold is excellent. There is also the bent-out point, as in the O'Shaughnessy design.

Few fishermen realize it, but hook sizes are far from standard, even though many books show actual sizes in drawings. Sizes among manufacturers differ, and they also may differ among hook designs from the same manufacturer. Thus it is best to decide which styles and brands are most useful for your particular purposes, then check out the sizes just in those. Once you know what you want, you have only to ask for or seek the needed sizes in favorite styles and brands.

The reason, incidentally, that I have not stated unequivocally which hook designs are best is that there is really no such thing as "best." The type of water, kind of bait used, type of tackle, fish species all dictate which hooks will be most efficient. More important, perhaps, than all of those is the whim of the individual fisherman. Talk to experienced bait fishermen and you'll soon discover most have very strong feelings about hook types. My foregoing descriptions and pointers, therefore, should serve only as guidelines. Trial and error in your particular fishing situation will reveal which ones work best for you.

Sinkers

A basic rule of thumb is to use the smallest sinker that will do the required job. Sinkers of course have only one fundamental purpose: to hold the bait at a given level. A live minnow fished without a sinker will usually come to the surface and be ineffective except in specialized situations, such as under hyacinth beds in Florida and other Deep South states. But a sinker used with any live bait should be just heavy enough to keep the bait at least near the selected level, yet not inhibit its movement. Certain rigs, as we'll see, assist in giving such baits free areas of motion. Nonetheless, always use the smallest, that is, lightest sinker that will do what is required of it and you will keep the inhibitions of biting fish to a minimum.

Sinkers have come a long way from the stove-bolt nut or bent nail of my boyhood. Although not as varied as hooks, sinkers nowadays have been developed to do numerous special bait-fishing duties. There is nothing very complicated about selecting the proper sinker for any situation. However, saltwater anglers need a broader selection of sinker designs than do their freshwater counterparts.

Split shot. This is a truly ingenious little lead device, used almost entirely in freshwater, although it has certain uses in saltwater in the bays and on the flats and in protected inside waters for light-tackle fishing. The split shot is precisely what its name implies—a small, round lead pellet split through the center about two-thirds of its diameter. It is pinched onto the line with pliers. Sizes differ among manufacturers but in general run from about BB size up to 00 buckshot. Size numbering may differ from firm to firm.

Probably the most ingenious refinements of the split shot have been introduced by Water Gremlin Company of White Bear Lake, Minnesota. Some seasons back they introduced the easily removable split shot. It can be secured without pliers because of the way the cut faces are creased. It has two small ears molded onto the side opposite the split. Pinching these together with only the fingers loosens the crimped-on shot so that it can be removed and used again.

Split shots are available in sizes to suit most freshwater situations.

The ingeniously designed removable split shot from Water Gremlin.

The split shot can be used singly in any size or in multiples, which makes it a most important and broadly useful type of sinker. For example, several small shot strung along a line may under certain conditions lay a bait flat on bottom more naturally than a single large split shot of the same weight. Chiefly, however, the shot is used by freshwater stillfishermen employing any of a large number of baits, from crickets to live minnows, and with or without a float. It is also used with various tackle by casters to add barely enough weight to a baited hook to make it castable.

Wrap-on lead strips. Some years ago lead wire and strips of thin lead were popular as wrap-on sinker material. Some anglers still carry them for emergencies or special situations. A piece can be wrapped around the line snugly, or even around the eye of a hook. Wrap-on materials are not as satisfactory, however, as the various specialized sinkers, and they are inclined to pick up weeds.

Clinch sinker. These sinkers are available in various designs. Most are long, slender ovals. Most common is a style with a slot down the center of one side, and a wing thrusting up from each end and from opposite sides. The line is laid in the groove, and the lead wings are pinched over and down snugly into a cut-out space. This secures the sinker firmly.

If the clinch-on process is carefully done, the line is not injured. However, one fault of this sinker is that it can cause abrasions on monofil lines.

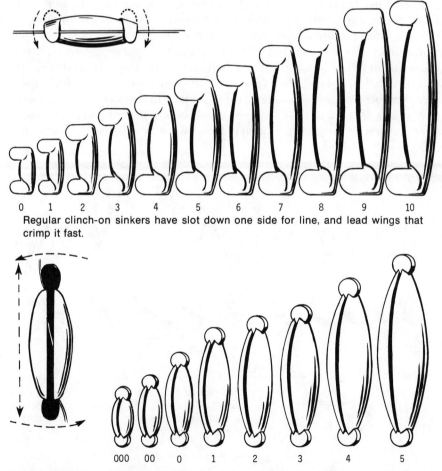

Regular clinch-on sinkers have slot down one side for line, and lead wings that crimp it fast.

Water Gremlin's Rubbercor clinch-on sinkers utilize strip of tough rubber that, when the protruding ears are twisted, holds firmly with no possible line abrasion.

An immense improvement in clinch sinkers is the Rubbercor (trademark). This one has no lead wings or ears to pinch closed. Instead, it has a strip of tough rubber forced down into the groove in the sinker, and small ears — the rounded ends of the strip — thrusting out from either end. Lay the line in the groove, exert a slight pull on the ears and twist them a half turn in. opposite directions. The sinker is then firmly in place. To remove, simply reverse the twist.

Clinch sinkers are useful for both bottom fishing and bobber fishing. They are also often used in small sizes instead of split shot, for stillfishing with a float or for casting a bait.

Dipsey sinker. This is a teardrop-shaped sinker with a loop of brass wire for an eye at the upper (smaller) end. The wire usually runs down through the center and is flattened at the bottom to hold it in place. In some cases it is secured inside. The design allows the sinker to swivel upon the stem. The shape of this extremely popular and useful sinker keeps to a minimum the chances of its fouling among rocks. It is used in varying sizes in a myriad ways: sometimes at the end of a line, with a baited dropper above it; sometimes tied in to the line above the baited hook; often in various three-way-swivel rigs (described in Part 2). Usually the dipsey is found in freshwater gear, but some larger ones — sizes from $1/8$ ounce to 8 ounces are available — find a place in saltwater. When used on a smooth bottom where current is strong, this style tumbles too much to be satisfactory — unless such tumbling is purposely desired.

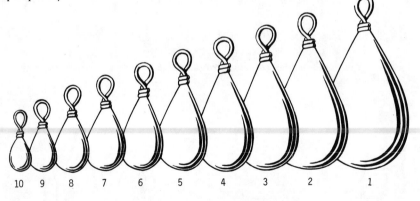

0

10   9   8   7   6   5   4   3   2   1

The regular type of dipsey (above), sometimes called a bell sinker. The Snap-Loc dipsey (left) is a patented design from Water Gremlin that is extremely handy.

A unique improvement on the dipsey is the Snap-Loc sinker, another innovation of one of the largest makers of sinkers, Water Gremlin Company. The swiveling device and its tie-on loop are formed of tough, moderately pliable plastic. The loop has a partition down its center, so there are two possible attachment methods. One side has a small locking slit in it. The sinker can simply be snapped onto the line, or onto the eye of a metal swivel or leader snap, with no tying. It can thus be attached instantly to any rig needing weight. This Snap-Loc side of the loop is used also for free-line fishing (see Part 2). The other side of the loop can be used of course in the traditional tie-on or loop-on manner.

Slip sinker. This is available in several styles, the most common of which is the egg sinker. It is roughly egg-shaped but rounded on each end. Another style is the teardrop, which is exactly like the dipsey but without the swivel and loop. All slip sinkers have a hole through the center. They are used chiefly in freshwater but sometimes in salt. The line is run through the hole. A live bait may thus wander, and a biting fish feels little or no resistance. Slip sinkers are used for casting, for bottom fishing, and with some rigs for trolling and drifting.

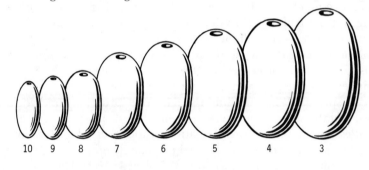

The egg slip sinker is designed to slide freely on the line. The bullet-shaped slip sinker was developed for plastic worm fishing but works just as well for night crawlers, and slips easily through debris.

A modern variation is the bullet-shaped slip sinker with a hollowed-out bottom used by almost all plastic-worm fishermen. The hollow in the bottom fits neatly over the head of the plastic worm and the buried eye of the hook. Because of its bullet shape, this sinker is not as prone to hang-ups in debris as the egg-shaped variety. Bait fishermen will find it well adapted as a free-line slip sinker for use with night crawlers and numerous other baits, as well as for casting and trolling.

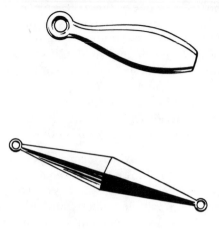

Bank sinkers are usually used in salt-water. The diamond design (bottom) is generally used for trolling.

Bank sinker. This one is used chiefly in saltwater. It is a club-shaped sinker with an eye molded in. It is used for bottom fishing where current is not strong, and for trolling. For years this general design was used – and still is in some instances – for salmon trolling offshore in the Pacific. Weighing a pound or more, to take a bait deep and keep it there, it is rigged to a sinker release. This mechanism ties in between line and leader. The hook-up for the sinker is at one side, and the interior of the release has a locking device and two springs. When a salmon strikes, the springs are pulled, the lock opens, and the sinker, considered expendable, drops, leaving the fish on a weightless line to offer a proper battle without the risk of tearing out the hook. The so-called downrigger used extensively nowadays in Great Lakes salmon fishing (see Part 2) has largely replaced this sinker.

Trolling and casting sinkers. The diamond is a simple design usually used for trolling. It is long, slender, and diamond-shaped, with a tie ring on each end, so it can be used between line and leader. It is sometimes used, with a hook at one end, as a jigging sinker in saltwater.

Many types of trolling and casting sinkers are available in slender, rounded torpedo shape for both fresh and salt. These usually have a swivel at one end and a snap at the other. Some have bead chain at each end along with a snap and a tie ring. These sinkers are designed to fit between the baited hook on its leader and the end of the line, and to have little water resistance. Types with swivel devices at both ends are best, to avoid twist. The keel sinker is a variation of the above used mostly for trolling. The bead chain or swivel and snap arrangements are the same, but the torpedo-shaped lead is fitted with a lead keel. The purpose of this design is to avoid line twist.

Torpedo-shaped trolling and casting sinkers are of several types. One variety has swivel at one end, snap at the other. Some have swivels or bead-chain at each end plus snap and tie rings. The keel trolling sinker (bottom) is a variation designed to keep line from twisting.

Pyramid sinker. The pyramid is probably the sinker most used in saltwater, particularly among surf and pier fishermen. It is a pyramid of solid lead, with flat sides and bottom. The purpose of this design is to hold well on various types of bottoms, especially where strong currents run. It is used in a variety of rigs. Some pyramid sinkers have the eye at the top or peak. These are used on rough bottoms. Others have the eye in the center of the flat bottom and are used on soft bottoms so that the peak buries itself. Some are available with tie-on eyes both top and bottom, for interchangeable use.

Pyramid sinkers are much used in saltwater. They have tie-up ring at top, bottom, or both. Which end you tie depends upon the bottom.

FOR ROUGH BOTTOM   FOR SOFT BOTTOM

Other sinkers. Regional sinker types are popular on various fishing fronts and are used in scattered locations. One most useful design is the so-called snagless or leaf sinker. It is a fairly thin, flat design usually with a teardrop outline and with the eye molded in. It does not hang up easily among rocks or bottom debris. It can be used at line's end, or tied in a stationary position. Or it can be used as a slip sinker. A variation on this general type that

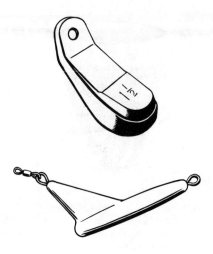

The snagless, or leaf, sinker (top); the walking sinker developed by Lindy Tackle (above right); and the drail.

has become quite popular of late is commonly called the "walking" sinker. This is molded so that the portion with the eye is bent inward slightly at an angle to the main body. This angle allows the main bulk of the flat sinker to "walk" along bottom and over obstacles. It is used either affixed in a selected position, or as a sliding sinker through which line can run free.

The drail presumably originated for deep saltwater fishing, as for cod, in the Northeast. The main body is a more or less torpedo-shaped piece of lead, but from the top and just past the midsection on one end a thick wing or upright keel thrusts out. There is a tie ring at either end of the sinker. The drail's waving motion when trolled or held on a snug line after being cast relays the slightest bite and possibly adds attractive motion to the bait. Occasionally the drail is used by surf fishermen.

Almost all fishermen prefer drab sinkers in their natural dull lead finish. Very occasionally, however, local tradition for certain bottom-feeding fish, generally in saltwater, is to paint the sinker. Supposedly a bright color is an attractor. Whether this really works, or is simply a regional whim, no one can say for certain.

Floats

Floats, or bobbers, have some specialized diversity, but there is nothing very complicated about selecting or using them. As with sinkers, a good rule is to use the smallest float that will properly do the required job. This avoids unduly arousing suspicion in the quarry, which may feel the resistance of the line.

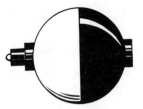

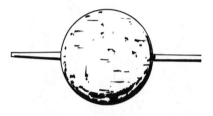

A common shape of cork bobber (above) with hole through the center and a wooden pin to hold the line. The clip-on plastic float (above right) can be simply clipped to line, or line can be run through the wire loop on one side and then through the clip. Big cork floats (right), unpainted, are sometimes used by northern muskellunge fishermen.

The float is used of course chiefly to suspend a bait at a desired level. The reason may be to keep the bait barely off bottom, or to keep it just above or beside a weed bed, in stillfishing. Long ago bottle corks and whittled bobbers of light wood were used, and later on cork floats were made in various designs. Today, for most freshwater fishing and much in salt, the bobber is of plastic. Most plastic floats clip onto the line with a spring and clip device and are thus easily adjustable for depth.

There are a few specialized floats for specific purposes. In the muskie country of the North a good many old hands still use baseball-sized round cork floats, often unpainted, when fishing suckers of a pound or more for muskellunge. Ice fishermen have available one of the most unique floats ever conceived. It was invented, I believe, by the Dickey Tackle Company of Land O' Lakes, Wisconsin. These floats are made of closed-cell sponge

Bobber of closed cell sponge rubber devised by Dicky Tackle Co. for ice fishing—when water freezes on it, just squeeze it. Small ones are fine for summer panfishing, too.

The so-called popping cork, used mostly in saltwater.

rubber. They are very light, to fit the weak bite of winter fish. Any bobber used in an ice hole soon becomes coated, on most days, with ice. To remove it on these sponge-rubber floats, all you have to do is pinch the bobber.

In saltwater the most important specialized float is the so-called "popping cork." It is used for weakfish—called sea trout or speckled trout in the South—as they feed on shrimp on the flats. It is a fairly long, cone-shaped bobber with a hole through it and a device thrust in that holds the line. The small end of the bobber is usually weighted. The top face is dished out. A shrimp is suspended below (see Part 2 for details on this rig), and when the rod tip is twitched, the dish-faced cork makes a slurping or popping sound, to simulate surface-feeding trout. The sound and the shrimp dancing below as the cork is popped together draw the fish.

Large, fat, egg-shaped bobbers, often of painted cork, are commonly used by tarpon fishermen who use live pinfish and other such baits in saltwater. Pier fishermen also often use sizable floats. Commonly a rig with a float is used along a pier or bridge over saltwater to fish down-current as a tide or the waves move. It drifts a bait along close to the pilings as the angler pays out line—unless of course there are other anglers in the line of drift whose rigs might be fouled.

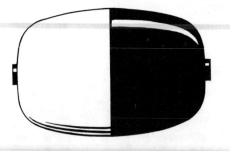

Large, oval-shaped bobbers are often used in saltwater, particularly by tarpon fishermen.

In some stores you may find casting floats that are self-adjustable, but they are not available everywhere. They are ingenious designs that slip down near the hook as the cast is made, so no awkward length of dangling line with sinker and bait has to be swung as a whole unit during the cast. Then as the bait sinks to the desired depth, a jerk on the line, or a preset device on the bobber, causes it to stop sliding up the line. Some of these designs work pretty well, some don't. More common and efficient is a bobber-stop arrangement that fits on the line at the desired fishing depth. The bobber slides down against the hook when the cast is made, but slips back up again until it hits the stopper once bait and sinker go down (see Part 2).

The casting bubble is something quite different. It is either round or tear-shaped and generally of clear plastic. The main purpose of the casting bubble is to give one enough weight to cast, with light spinning tackle as a rule, a baited hook with a very light sinker or none at all. To achieve this, the bubble is designed so that it can be filled partly full of water. It has a waterproof plug or stopper. An eyedropper is a handy gadget for putting the water in. Some specialists use mineral oil, but this is not necessary.

Obviously, the more liquid there is in the bubble, the greater the weight, and the lower the bubble rides in the water. The bubble allows you to cast a bait just as you'd cast a lure. It also allows a slow retrieve of the dangling bait, at a desired depth and on a path guided by the adeptness of the angler. It is even possible (see Part 2) to rig up with a properly placed sinker and put in enough liquid to make the bubble sink and stay barely above bottom, holding the bait there. Perhaps this isn't using the bubble as a float in the true sense, because you don't watch it for indication of a bite. But it does illustrate the versatility of this little device.

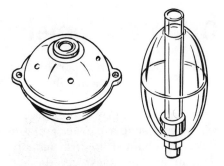

Casting bubbles come in several shapes and designs, can be filled partially with water to add casting weight. They have many uses.

Undoubtedly you will run across other types of floats here and there. I remember an expert carp-fisherman friend who used quill floats because of their ultralightness. I myself have as a kind of conversation piece a bundle of quill floats made from the viciously sharp, long quills of the African crested porcupine. They are so light no sinker or only a small shot can be used with them. The slightest nudge of a bait on bottom jiggles the quill on surface. I might add that these quills are so hard and sharp they are really a

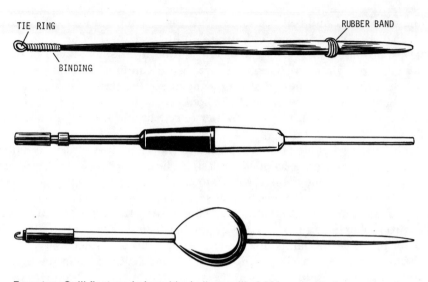

TIE RING

BINDING

RUBBER BAND

From top: Quill float made from big, hollow quill of African crested porcupine; two plastic quill-type bobbers. The line secures to one end, and they tip up at a bite.

little dangerous to carry. No bait fisherman really needs such tricked-up floats, and those already described are the basic and most useful ones available.

Other Equipment

Swivels and snaps are a part of the bait fisherman's equipment, but the astute angler will use them only when absolutely necessary. The reason is that fish can be mightily inhibited by oddments of terminal tackle when they are not avidly feeding. As an example, one time on the Texas coast during a winter cold snap a partner and I fished live shrimp on bottom in a deep hole in a channel. Redfish (channel bass) and speckled weakfish (trout) gang up in deep holes when the water temperature drops low. The competition for food is then severe, but the metabolism of the fish is slowed substantially, and bites are most tentative.

I was using a spinning outfit and had tied my hook directly to the line. My partner, who on most occasions managed to outfish me, used a snap-and-swivel at line's end and attached the hook to it. I caught fish after fish, crawling the shrimp very slowly across bottom. He had not a single nip. The only obvious difference in our rigs was his snap-and-swivel. He removed it—and began matching me.

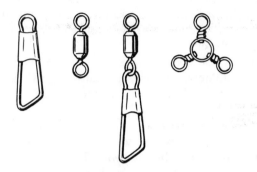

Snaps and swivels come in many designs. Basically there are four main ones (from left): snaps alone; swivels alone; swivel and snap together; three-way swivel.

So, don't clutter up your terminal tackle unless you need to. Many rigs, however, require snaps and swivels, as we'll see in Part 2. You can buy snaps by themselves. They are devices of a safety-pinlike design—individual manufacturers' styles differ somewhat—with a ring to tie to the line and a snap to which the hook is attached. The snap in this instance serves only to facilitate hook changes without cutting the line. There are also swivels in various sizes with a tie ring on either end. The chief purpose of the swivel is to avoid line twist.

In addition to the snap and swivel by themselves, and more commonly used, are the combinations of swivel and snap together. In trolling, casting and retrieving bait, and for many bottom-fishing rigs these combination items are needed.

Another item in this equipment category that is much used, particularly in saltwater rigs, is the three-way swivel. It may best be described as a small metal band into the outer circumference of which three-eyed swivels are set at equal intervals. The purpose of the three-way swivel is to allow attachment of the line, a dropper with a sinker, and a dropper with baited hook, all from a central point, yet separated.

Swivels and snaps are finished in black, bronze, and in bright plating. The dull finishes are the most desirable because they are inconspicuous. In saltwater, however, bright plating to resist corrosion is much used. If you are fishing for active school fish such as any of the mackerels, be a bit wary of bright connections. These swift fish snap at any bright moving object and rather commonly cut lines when doing so.

Nowadays practically all freshwater bait fishermen use monofil lines. There is therefore very little need for leaders. In debris-filled waters bass fishermen use heavy monofil, which is not easily harmed. Trout and panfish fishermen need no leader of steel or heavier monofil than is on the reel. Many anglers after muskies, pike, and walleyes do use leaders, to keep the teeth of these fish from cutting the line. However, if you try to avoid letting a fish swallow the bait, and use heavy monofil, cut-offs will not often occur.

Whenever the habitat and the fish species allow, use no metal leader. But do keep a check on the last few inches of line. Rocks cause abrasions in freshwater. Snip off the roughed-up end of the line often and retie. In saltwater the situation is radically different. Shell beds, barnacles on pilings, the teeth and hard mouths of many fish species make some sort of leader mandatory much of the time. Fortunately, on the whole saltwater fish are not as skittish of unrefined terminal tackle as many freshwater varieties are — although, as already noted, there are exceptions.

The three main kinds of leaders for either salt or fresh are plain piano wire, braided wire, and braided wire with a covering of nylon. Piano-wire leaders are of smaller diameter than those of braided wire. But piano wire kinks unmercifully when a fish leaps or rolls during a battle, and sometimes even when it is carefully coiled. It is almost impossible to straighten. Thus braided wire is advantageous because it is more flexible. A nylon covering, though adding slightly to diameter, makes the braided wire still more flexible and nonkinkable, as well as rather unobtrusive.

Some fishermen may enjoy making up their own leaders. However, it is far easier to purchase ready-made ones. Almost all are fitted with a swivel at one end and a snap at the other. Braided wire, coated or uncoated, may be had in numerous lengths — 4, 6, 8, 9, 12, 18 inches. It can be used in either fresh- or saltwater. Several poundage strength tests are available. It is a good idea to always carry a supply in your box, but again, use wire leaders only when really necessary. Trolling leaders for large fish are generally long — 6 feet or more — and made of so-called piano wire.

When trolling or casting and retrieving bait, almost all anglers employ a spinner or spinners ahead of the bait as an attractor. There are, as everyone knows, scores of different designs. Among the most popular blade styles for freshwater are the Colorado spinner, the June Bug spinner, and the Indiana in single or twin blades. Long strings of spinners in diminishing size are used by some anglers, especially for trout trolling. Sometimes a spinner with a swivel to attach it to the line, and another below with a treble hook on it — the Colorado style — are simply baited and cast or trolled. Other spinners are often attached to a length of monofil and trail the bait a short distance behind. Some of these rigs will be described in Part 2. Many of them can be bought economically already made up. Most spinner use is in freshwater, although some large attractors — called flashers or dodgers — are used for certain saltwater endeavors.

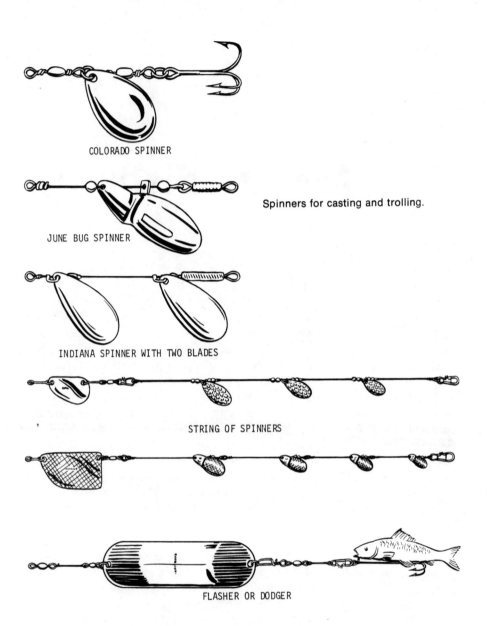

COLORADO SPINNER

JUNE BUG SPINNER

Spinners for casting and trolling.

INDIANA SPINNER WITH TWO BLADES

STRING OF SPINNERS

FLASHER OR DODGER

31

PART 2

Rigs for Bait Fishing

WHEN BAIT FISHERMEN speak of a "rig," they refer to the arrangement and variety of the terminal tackle. Some rigs use a float, many do not. Some call for swivels, snaps, and spinners in addition to hook and sinker. Others utilize only a hook and sinker, and some are utter simplicity—only a hook. In Part 1 the several components, their varieties, and specific uses were explained. A rig, then, is a selection of certain components of equipment that are terminally attached in an arrangement that best suits the angler's purpose and location, and that has generally proved effective from past experience.

Fundamentally, the purpose of most fishing rigs is to utilize the several simple categories of equipment in combinations that will allow the bait to be presented and held at a given depth. To that end some allow fishing near surface, others at any depth between surface and bottom. Many are designed for bottom fishing, or placing the bait at least very close to bottom, for this is where many fish forage much of the time.

Some rigs are designed chiefly for fishing living bait that moves on its own. Others are used with bait either alive or dead. Some of the most successful bottom-fishing and near-bottom rigs are ingeniously contrived to allow a live bait to roam over a modest area on its tether, or to enable currents to move any tethered bait temptingly. Others employ a heavy sinker up the line above a small submerged float, so that the bait is lifted off bottom slightly, thus keeping it out of debris. Among the most popular and productive of all bottom rigs are those that use slip sinkers. Live bait moves more freely, current moves dead bait at will, and moreover a fish picking up the bait feels no pressure on the line. These rigs bear various names in various places, but "fish finder" and "free-line" are the terms most commonly attached to them.

The variety of bait rigs is probably greater for saltwater than for freshwater. This is because, as noted earlier, bait is much more extensively used and for more varied species in saltwater. However, standard setups do not differ radically between the two mediums. That is, the arrangement of the several components for any given type of rig is about the same, but heavier materials are generally used in saltwater, and another kind of sinker or hook may be substituted in salt for the one used in fresh. The type of bottom, or tidal currents, or the size and toughness of the fish dictate these switches.

The basic rigs for both mediums number no more than a dozen or so in all. But each has been endlessly personalized or regionalized by widely scattered anglers attempting to fit it more productively to specialized fishing situations. An individual angler tries one of the basic rigs and makes minor changes that he believes add effectiveness under his circumstances. Maybe the result becomes popular over his area and is given a localized name. But another angler hundreds of miles distant would instantly recognize it as merely an adaptation of one he calls by another name.

As an example, I know an ice-fishing walleye addict in Wisconsin who experimented with the Kahle Horizontal hook mentioned in Part 1. Except for a switch to this odd hook, his rig is like any standard ice-fishing setup that uses minnows. The Kahle has not gained any great popularity, because most anglers are skeptical of its hooking ability. But this man became convinced that he missed fewer bites by using it. Thus he came to always utilize this hook in his standard rig. He has convinced friends locally of the effectiveness of his personal rig, which has consequently become a standard setup throughout his area.

Any minor switch from a so-called basic rig—a slightly different sinker placement or sinker type, the use, or absence, of a swivel—becomes a new and personalized design. Thus over the years probably hundreds of terminal arrangements have evolved. It would be impossible to list and describe all of them. From the well-known proven and popular rigs covered here, however, anyone can and should branch out to try new arrangements of his own. Often, as I've said, the habitat situation of a particular fish species in a certain latitude may dictate changes that will be advantageous, at least locally. And who knows, the "improved" rig that you contrive regionally to lick a certain problem may find a place in fishing history one of these days as a standard for that particular use.

The descriptions of rigs in the following pages do not deal with the way to place specific kinds of bait on the hook, or in fact with the detailed techniques of fishing various baits. Their immediate purpose is simply to show how to arrange the terminal tackle components to form the various basic combinations.

Freshwater Rigs

A sharp way to use split shot for a variety of fishing endeavors is to attach a very short dropper and pinch the shot very lightly on it. If the shot gets hung, a steady pull will strip it off, and you don't lose the entire rig. It may

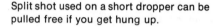

Split shot used on a short dropper can be
pulled free if you get hung up.

be properly said that a selection of split shot in varied sizes is one of the
most important items in the tacklebox of the freshwater bait angler, and
that the inshore saltwater fisherman should certainly have at least a modest
collection for specialized light-tackle occasions.

The most fundamental of all freshwater setups is the one invented cen-
turies ago by the long-pole stillfisherman and only slightly changed in principle (although a good deal in refinement of tackle) to this day. It consists of
a float attached to the line at a selected distance from the hook, so that the
bait will be presented at a preselected depth. In addition to the float, a small
weight is attached to the line a few inches above the hook. The usual sinker
for this work nowadays is the split shot. One or more, of a size needed to
hold the bait at proper depth, are used. If a heavier sinker is required,
usually one of the clinch types is selected.

This simple rig of course has now been in use, with some variations, for
many years among fishermen using baitcasting, spinning, and even fly
rods. In general floats for this use are one of two types. One has a hole
through its center, through which the line is threaded. A slender round
plug made of wood or a length of plastic is thrust into the hole to secure the
line. The other type utilizes a small, U-shaped metal clip, open on one side
and usually operated by a push button on a spring on the opposite side of
the float. The device clips the line snugly to a groove in the float. Obviously,
either of these floats can be adjusted quickly and easily for more or less
depth.

34

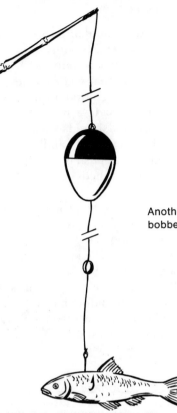

Another basic freshwater arrangement: bobber, sinker, baited hook.

The problem presented to the fisherman who intends to cast this rig, however, is one of awkwardness. Let's suppose you wish to fish at a depth of 3 feet. With the bobber set at that depth, you must swing the entire setup in a sidewinder swing. If the sinker is very light — a single split shot perhaps — the float outweighs it, and tangles are common. Also, in close quarters foul-ups are common.

To lick this problem, a sliding float can be used. The type with the hole through the middle is simply used without the plug thrust in to secure the line. Others have a small ring of metal or plastic attached to the side through which the line freely slides. Thus prior to the cast the float has slipped down and is resting against the sinker, only a few inches from the bait. Obviously there has to be a stopper arrangement up the line at the desired depth, so that after the cast, as the sinker takes the bait down, the bobber stops at a predetermined distance above the bait.

Several firms have patented small devices of one kind or another to accomplish this, and there have been innumerable, somewhat complicated bobbers marketed that will stop their slide at a preset length up the line. Many were too complicated and faded from the scene. Others may not always be readily available in tackle stores. So, you should know how to contrive your own stop system. I believe the best way is as follows.

Almost all fishermen nowadays use monofil lines. Snip off a few inches, 6 or 8, from your line. Leaving one free end of an inch or more, wrap this snippet four or five times around your line a couple of feet or so up from its end. Leave the coils rather loose, so that you can then tuck each end, from opposite directions of course, through under the coils and pull them snug, slowly and gently. You've thus made a multiple-coil knot around your line. It should be pulled tight, but it should also be movable. Try sliding it up or down a bit, holding the line straight and tight meanwhile. Get the tension set so that a modest amount of push is required to slide the knot in either direction. When that is accomplished, snip the ends off as close as possible.

You may have to experiment a bit to get the process down pat. If, for example, you are using a very fine line, perhaps you'll need to use mono of a size or so larger to make this sliding knot, since fine lines aren't so adaptable to this method as heavier ones. After the knot is finished, slide a bead onto the end of the line. Plastic beads with a hole through them can be found in most tackle stores. They're used on numerous spinner rigs and with other lures. Below the bead the free-sliding bobber is strung on. Then the split shot or clinch sinker is placed wherever you want it above the bait but below the bobber, and the hook is tied on.

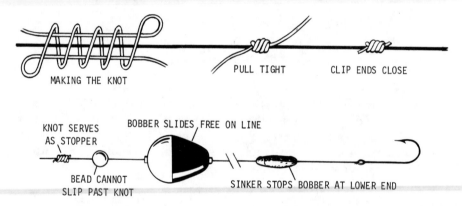

MAKING THE KNOT　　　PULL TIGHT　　　CLIP ENDS CLOSE

KNOT SERVES AS STOPPER　　BOBBER SLIDES FREE ON LINE

BEAD CANNOT SLIP PAST KNOT　　SINKER STOPS BOBBER AT LOWER END

Now as you hold the rig up, dangling it from the end of the rod, the bobber is resting against the sinker, a few inches up from the baited hook. The bead rests atop the bobber. The knot has been slipped to a predetermined depth measurement. It is up inside the guides of your rod somewhere. Seldom will you need to fish with the bobber at a depth greater than the length of your rod plus the portion of line that hangs off the end with float, sinker, and hook. In this way the stop-knot on the line does not get to the reel, and it will slide easily through the rod guides when you cast.

Thus you are casting the aggregate weight of baited hook, sinker, and float all gathered at one general point. As the sinker carries the bait down after the cast, the bobber slides up the line, shoving the bead ahead of it. When the bead hits the knot, it stops and also stops the float from sliding farther. If you want greater or lesser depth, simply slide the knot up or down the line. The trick of course is to get just the right tension on the sliding knot, so that it does not slip when the float hits it, or when a fish takes the float under. That's not difficult.

Although this is in my opinion the best bobber-casting rig, I confess that I don't always bother to make it up. When I am fishing where there is ample side-swing casting room, as from a boat or from the open bank of a pond, and not fishing more than 2 or 3 feet deep, I simply pinch on a split shot, clip a bobber to the line and have at it. It's far more awkward, granted, but it's fast when a fellow is eager to get catching fish, especially in the panfish category.

In Part 1, I briefly described the casting bubble. The standard float or bobber is intended in most cases to be very light. Even though small, light ones can be cast when rigged as described, particularly with spinning tackle, the bubble, designed to be partially filled with water or other liquid, is a gadget for adding actual casting weight. Most are designed so that they retrieve more easily and with less surface commotion than the standard float. And they are very useful when you want to make up a rig using either no sinker at all, or else a very small split shot.

Originally the bubble was created to allow spin- or baitcasting fishermen to cast artificial flies and other nearly weightless lures. But its advantages for use with small baits are substantial. For example, I have often rigged up for panfish by using a very light hook and a small worm or cricket, and no sinker. The bubble can be tied in to the line at a preselected depth, or used with the free-sliding setup already described. For large bluegills, for instance, that are extra-shy, a small bait with no weight seen wafting down on a free fall through the water is most persuasive. For this use it is obviously best to tie the bubble at a preselected depth. With a small split shot it can be allowed to slide. The small sinker takes the bait down.

It should be noted that clear plastic bubbles seem, to fish below, to be nothing much, perhaps even air bubbles—or so their enthusiasts claim. Also, filling the bubble with water to the point where it just floats enables the angler to still see it but offers little resistance to a biting fish, because the bubble is then almost equal in density to water.

For fishing fairly shallow, say to a couple of feet, and with two or three shot, many enthusiasts of the casting bubble rig as follows: split shot a few inches above the baited hook; a bubble tied in to the line at a 2-foot depth. Or: a swivel as stopper 2 feet up the line; a bubble sliding free below, stopped at bottom by shot some inches above the baited hook.

As I mentioned in Part 1, the bubble is also used as a device simply to keep a bait barely above bottom. In this case it is not a float to be watched for evidence of a bite. The rig is made as follows: a clinch-type sinker is placed on the line 2 to 4 feet (or less as needed) from its end; the bubble is tied in to the line about midway between sinker and baited hook; the bubble can be partly filled with water, or used empty, depending on how buoyant you want the bait to be.

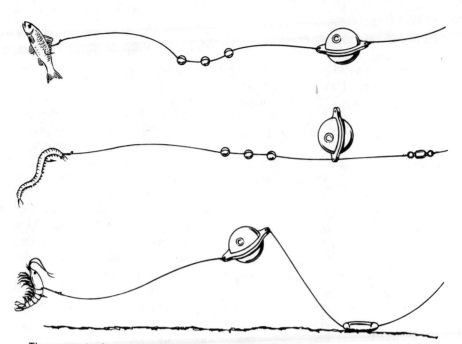

Three ways to rig a casting bubble. Top, a shallow-water setup with split shot, bubble tied on two feet above bait. Center, bubble slides on line, split shot below and swivel above. Bottom: Bubble used underwater to buoy bait off bottom; clinch sinker holds line on bottom.

This rig is a bit awkward to cast because of its length. Once cast, however, the sinker lies on bottom while the bubble rises well off bottom. This in turn raises the bait, which floats free with no weight attached close to it. Obviously the sinker used must be large enough so that the bubble can't raise it. All of these bubble rigs are excellent for stream as well as lake fishing. When cast up and across a current they allow the bait to float in a semifree and enticing state as the weight and the bubble tumble along.

Use of a float rig is not confined to stillfishing and casting. Simple float rigs are used for drifting, as for example when fishing for pike or muskellunge with large minnows, and also for varied bait fishing when a boat is rowed or paddled very slowly. There is nothing complicated that needs describing about such rigs. All you have to remember is that the sinker must be large enough to keep a live bait down where you want it to be, and in turn the bobber must be large enough so that this bait can't pull it under and keep it there, although it is certainly acceptable to use a size that a large minnow can pull around and even momentarily submerge.

For a great many bait-fishing endeavors, the simplest setup of all is the most effective. This means fishing without a float, and if possible without a sinker, or at the most with only the lightest sinker needed to cast the bait. It

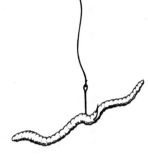

The simplest setup of all and sometimes the most effective: casting a bait without a float and with no sinker or the smallest one possible.

is surprising how easily and effectively worms and night crawlers can be cast with light spin tackle, the former with only a single small shot, the latter commonly with no added weight at all. The effectiveness of course is because the bait wafts down in a perfectly natural manner.

If the bottom is clear, the bait can be allowed to sink right down. If there are weeds or other debris on bottom, the angler must judge how far to let the bait sink and how to maneuver it from there on. As a classic example, during the spawning season for bluegills I recently fished with very light spinning gear, using crickets for bait and a single small split shot. We found bedding areas by trial and error, anchored over a sand and small-gravel bottom in about 10 feet of water, which was what the fish had selected. That is too deep for practical use of a float, and anyway we needed to have the bait on bottom. With the light spinning tackle we could cast as far as we needed to, and we sacked up dozens of big males that were gathering to fan beds.

Whenever you can use such utterly simple setups productively, by all means do so. The rule of thumb should always be to clutter up terminal tackle as little as possible. As the need occurs, however, one must add items of tackle, or vary their arrangement. Basically, after the float is eliminated, bait rigs are almost entirely based on the use and placement of various types of sinkers, plus the addition perhaps of swivels, snaps, and spinners.

In a rig I use a great deal for many species of freshwater fish, the sinker is placed at the end of the line and a dropper tied in 8 inches to a foot or more above. The sinker type most commonly used is the dipsey. Most descriptions of this basic rig recommend the use of a three-way swivel as the connecting point. That is, a swivel is tied to the end of the line, and a short length of monofil is tied to each of the other rings, one used for the hook, the other for the sinker.

The three-way swivel of course affords an easy way to make the rig, and it helps to avoid tangles. Nevertheless, I like my own method better, even though there is some spiraling of the dropper around the sinker section. I tie the dipsey—of the smallest size consistent with the habitat situation and the type of bait to be used—directly to the end of the line. Eight inches or so from its end, I double the line to make a short loop between the thumb

39

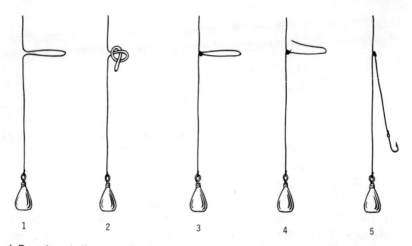

1. Form loop in line at desired distance above sinker and hold with thumb and forefinger. 2. Tie triple overhand knot, with three twists to form multiple tie. Sketch shows first time end is looped through; repeat twice more. 3. Pull knot tight, leaving loop extending from line. 4. Snip off one strand of loop close to multiple knot, to form dropper line. 5. Finished rig with hook attached. I make this rig up so dropper is shorter than knot to sinker distance, to keep bait just off bottom.

and forefinger of my left hand. I then draw this loop out longer, taking the extra line from that leading to the rod, so as to keep the distance from loop to sinker the same.

With a loop about 6 inches long, I then tie three square knots at its base, close to where I'm holding the doubled line, piling one knot atop another. Once this multiple knot is pulled tight, I can snip one side of the loop off close to the knot. The knot will hold firm for fish such as panfish, bass, and any medium-sized species. I then cut back the dropper length thus formed from the loop to make sure it is slightly shorter than the distance from knot to sinker. For most baits, habitats, and fishing methods I find this works best and creates less tangles.

There are two chief ways to use this rig. One is for fishing vertically, as over the side of a boat or from a bridge. The sinker is let down until it touches bottom. The line is then snugged up until it is barely tight, so that the bait is positioned just off bottom. If alive it can move a bit, and if not, it is still easily seen by fish. If there is any current, it waves back and forth. The slightest nudge of a fish is easily felt because no sinker interferes.

The second productive method of using this setup is casting it. It is especially effective on smooth bottoms, along the bottom at the fringes of weed beds, and in all such places where few hang-ups are likely and weeds or debris won't collect on the hook. I recall a lake in northern Michigan loaded with bass and big bluegills that were hard to find and catch in summer. Much of the bottom was soft and with few weeds, but loaded with aquatic nymphs and various worms. I'd cast and then reel very slowly. The dipsey sinker, dragging easily along such a bottom, left a tiny trail of mud, which caught fish attention. The method was deadly. It works very well in streams, too, if you cast downstream and retrieve slowly. The bait then waves in current near bottom.

Casting the dipsey dropper rig and retrieving slowly along smooth bottoms or near weed beds is a telling method.

This rig has several variations. Some anglers put the sinker on a section of line much shorter than the bait dropper, use minnows and fish vertically over the boat side. The minnow thus has much more roaming area near bottom. Yellow-perch fishermen make up similar rigs, with or without three-way swivels, and commonly use two droppers for baited hooks, spaced perhaps a foot apart. For fish that are not likely to be skittish, some fishermen make up these rigs with either one or two droppers and use quite stiff, heavy nylon for the entire rig. It is then connected to the lighter-test fishing line by a standard swivel. The heavier mono for the rig helps avoid tangles.

Two-dropper bottom rig with sinker on short leader gives minnows or other live bait ample roaming freedom at two levels near bottom.

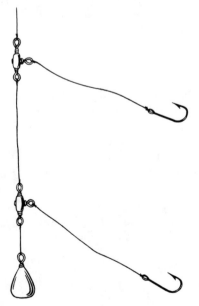

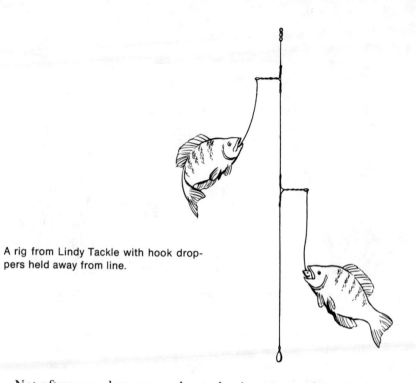

A rig from Lindy Tackle with hook droppers held away from line.

Not often seen, but extremely productive, are panfish bait rigs that use wire to help hold the bait dropper out away from the line and sinker section. Occasionally these are available in tackle stores. One type (made by Lindy Tackle) has a length of fairly stiff monofil (or fine wire) with a swivel at the upper end and a snap at the lower. Spaced well apart down the length are two stiff, short wire arms extending out horizontally. To each a snelled hook is attached. The line is tied to the upper swivel, and a dipsey sinker is snapped to the bottom. This setup is of course fished straight down, the sinker barely touching bottom or suspended, as the situation and species require.

There is also the device called a spreader. This is a piece of stiff wire, either straight or curved, that has a tie-on eye or swivel at its center, and places to attach snelled hooks at either end. These are occasionally used for stillfishing, generally for schooling varieties that are not shy, so that two hooks can help haul 'em in fast. A unique type of spreader I saw recently is available from the mail-order firm of Herter's, Inc., Waseca, Minnesota. It is a length of wire down-curved at either end that has a lead weight with a line-tie eye set in at its center. At each end there are coiled-spring clips to which hooks, snelled or regular, can be attached. The center lead carries the device to the desired depth and eliminates any chance of tangles.

As I said earlier, the slip-sinker setup called the fish-finder rig or a method of free-lining is one of the most useful of all combinations. In Part 1 the section entitled "Sinkers" noted the types most used in freshwater for this purpose. They are the egg sinker, the dipsey, and the snagless and walking sinkers. There are even shot available with a hole instead of a split

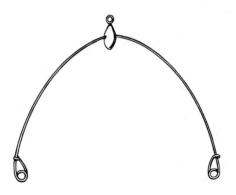

There are several types of spreaders. This one has weight at the center.

to make ultralight free-lining rigs. The slip-sinker concept is to get the bait down on or near bottom by using a weight that touches bottom, but without tying the sinker to the line. This allows a living bait to wander a little. But its main advantage with any bait is when fish are shy or biting lightly. When the bait is picked up, the line slides through the sinker or its eye. The angler lets off slack, and the fish is allowed to run or move off with the bait. As a rule of thumb, when it stops, the bait is being taken deep into the mouth, and the hook can be set.

There is nothing complicated about putting the fish finder together. You need a stopper of some sort so that the sinker does not slip clear down against the baited hook. Some anglers use a standard swivel anywhere from 6 inches to a couple of feet above the hook. This tends to avoid any line twist if a bait is alive. It stops the sinker effectively, which is up the line above it, yet casting is not much inhibited by this short hang-over of the rig from the rod tip. Some fishermen simply pinch on a small split shot as a stopper at the required distance above the baited hook.

After the cast is made the line should be reeled up so there is only the slightest tension. Slack should be readily available. The nibble of a fish is easily felt. If it moves off with the bait, slack is offered at the mildest tension so that the angler can keep track of what's happening but not inhibit the quarry until he judges it is time to set the hook. That's all there is to it.

Among the most artful forms of bait fishing is that of fishing salmon eggs, singly or in skeins or clusters, for trout and salmon. Innumerable rigs have been conceived for these endeavors. You will find details about attaching the baits, and about how to do the fishing, in Part 3 under the

The free-line, or fish-finder, rig with a single salmon egg. Preferably, leader should be lighter than line.

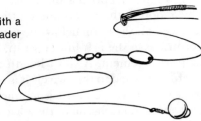

salmon-egg heading. The basic rig used by most anglers is purely and simply the free-line or fish finder, consisting of an egg sinker slipping freely on the line, a swivel as a stopper, and a leader anywhere from 2 to 4 feet long. Preferably the leader should be of mono lighter than the line, and just as light as the fish you're after will allow. For example, some anglers after moderate-sized trout use 6-pound test line, and a leader of half that or even 1- or 2-pound test. For big steelhead or salmon, obviously you have to have a heavier leader.

The same setup can be used of course for fishing an egg sac or cluster. But an ingenious hook rig is often employed for these. The leader is run through the eye of the hook and is tied securely and very tightly midway down the shank. Often an Eagle Claw Bait Holder hook in short or medium shank is used, and the leader is tied below the shank bait-holder barb so that it won't slip up. This tie leaves a loop between shank and eye, which can be opened wide and placed around the cluster and then pulled tight.

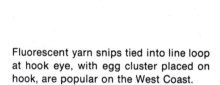

Method of tying line to hook so an egg cluster can be snugged into loop. With Bait Holder hooks, the tie is made below the shank barb.

Fluorescent yarn snips tied into line loop at hook eye, with egg cluster placed on hook, are popular on the West Coast.

Very popular and deadly also are rigs that originated on the West Coast rivers among steelheaders. A couple of short lengths of fluorescent yarn in pink, red, or yellow are wrapped around the top of the hook as attractors and secured by a loop in the mono line that is pulled tight at the eye. An egg cluster is placed on the hook below the yarn. There is a swivel between line and leader just as in the fish-finder setup, but this rig usually utilizes a different sinker arrangement. A short length of surgical tubing is slipped onto the line before it is tied to the swivel. It is placed 12 to 18 inches up the line, and a piece of pencil-sized lead is jammed into it. I did not mention pencil leads among sinkers because they are so seldom used except for highly specialized regional purposes such as this.

As can be seen, this sinker attachment places the weight in a nonslip position. The idea is to use it in swift streams and have it bounce and tumble along the bottom while the bait waves and swirls naturally. Pencil leads are available from tackle shops that carry such rigs. Whether this rig hangs up more — certainly many are lost — than the standard slip-sinker setup is hard to say. In any case, this is a unit much used by West Coast steelheaders. There are many variations on the setup just described, some of them even using three-way swivels, but the one noted here is the basic arrangement.

In tackle stores bait anglers can find scores of ready-rigged hook, leader, and spinner combinations for a wide variety of fishing that hardly need detailed description here. An example is the well-known so-called "worm harness," in which as a rule three hooks are evenly spaced along a length of monofil, below a spinner and beads. The remainder of the rig consists of more monofil with a tie-on loop at the end. A big night crawler can be stretched out on the three hooks. Single-hook-and-spinner setups are legion. Double-bladed spinners above hooks are also abundantly available.

Ready-made rigs with hook, leader, and spinner combinations are available in tackle shops.

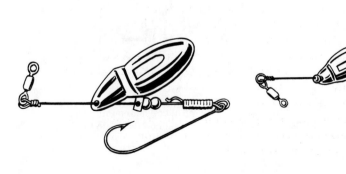

One of the all-time greats among these simple terminal rigs has long been the June Bug spinner, single or double blade, with a long bait hook directly attached by a snap or sliding spring clip behind it.

Other good bets at times are simple small spinners such as the Colorado with a treble hook and swivel attached immediately below. I recall that some years ago I used to fish the Sturgeon River in northern Michigan with a treble-hooked Colorado, and on some days the trout would avidly bat it with no bait added. On other days, however, I might not be able to induce a single fish until I draped some bait, usually a worm, on the treble. All of these popular and productive bait rigs are so commonly available in tackle shops that no more need be said of them here—except that their simplicity by no means detracts from their deadliness.

We do need to dwell briefly, however, on what has become known as the downrigger trolling device. In Part 1 under "Sinkers" I mentioned the sinker release mechanism used for some years on the West Coast for salmon trolling in saltwater. The idea was to use a heavy weight to take the bait down where the salmon were, maybe at 50 feet or more. When a fish struck, the sinker release opened and dropped the weight free and expendable. The fish was then held on a line without weight, where it could battle properly, and more importantly where the heavy weight could not tear the hook out.

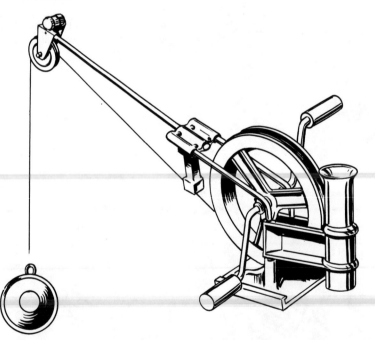

The downrigger device has revolutionized deep trolling at constant depth. It gained much of its present popularity because of its success in salmon fishing in the Great Lakes, where it was introduced a few years ago.

The downrigger, now used in both fresh- and saltwater, is a vast improvement. Its current renown is mostly a result of the phenomenal success of salmon in the Great Lakes, chiefly in Lake Michigan, and their immense popularity. It is a fairly expensive piece of equipment that properly belongs here, I believe, under freshwater rigs, even though it is gaining in salt. It is permanently affixed to the rail or transom of a craft of proper size for fishing the big water of the Great Lakes. A large single-action crank reel with an additional smaller pulley lets down or pulls up, vertically, a large trolling weight. This is either a ball or a vaned weight to keep it running straight. It may weigh as much as 10 pounds, since it must—or should—remain straight down while trolling.

Various downriggers utilize different release devices for the line. Basically, the idea is to clip the fisherman's line by such a device to a leader running out behind the weight. The cable to which the weight is attached is measured in feet or yards, so that it can be let down to an exact depth where fish are found to be lying. The angler pays off line from his reel as the weight goes down. Preferably the boat should be in motion meanwhile. Once the lure has reached the precise depth of the waiting fish—coho, lake trout, or chinook in Lake Michigan—it travels along at that depth, out behind the dangling weight at any distance deemed advisable.

When a fish strikes, it automatically hooks itself. That jolt releases the line. The angler has his bruiser with no weight attached. No big sinker is lost to the depths. But there are other advantages. The Pacific method in vogue some years back, which I described, put a great strain on the tackle and required the angler to hold on mightily, or prop his rod in a holder, because of the enormous drag of the big sinker down below. With the downrigger there is very little pull on the fishing line. In addition, the trolling depth can be precisely controlled instead of simply letting out line and weight by guesswork. The downrigger in fact has revolutionized salmon and lake-trout fishing in the Great Lakes and has become popular elsewhere.

Saltwater Rigs

In the introduction to this section I explained that possibly there was greater variety among rigs for saltwater because bait is used there for a greater variety of species. But I also noted that saltwater setups were not really very different in arrangement of components from those used in fresh. Only the type of the items differs. For example a different type of sinker may be used because of rugged currents, as in surf fishing. Thus, because freshwater rigging has been described in some detail, there is no need to repeat these descriptions, but only to call attention to some particular uses and modifications.

As a starting example, the same really ancient, simple combination of bobber and small sinker used by primitive anglers and in our day by cane-polers and some casters is useful for numerous saltwater endeavors. A clinch-type sinker or a small trolling sinker is used with the baited hook a few inches below it. A regular snap-on float is clipped to the line at the selected depth. This simple rig is handy for a broad variety of saltwater fishing in quiet inside waters. It is common, for instance, as a snook setup in tidal stream mouths around the Florida bays and is most useful for drifting over shallow weed-bed flats for speckled trout (weakfish).

I recall seeing it used by dozens of anglers on Florida bay bridges, all using baits of small minnows, when the Spanish mackerel were on the move early in spring. It is handy for all sorts of saltwater panfish fishing—grunts, various small snappers—and in fact for any fish variety that is not predominantly a bottom feeder and that frequents rather shallow water, so that the distance from float to bait need not be too awkward. On occasion some saltwater species fished by this method may require a swivel and wire leader below the sinker because of their teeth or rough mouths.

Ordinarily this arrangement is termed a surface rig. It is often used along piers and for drifting a bait temptingly on a slow current. It is essentially the same as the rig used by bait anglers after tarpon. I've seen the T-head of many a pier on the Texas Gulf Coast crowded with tarpon enthusiasts who fish this way, using large bobbers and suspending a live pinfish bait 6 feet or more below it.

The simple combo of bobber and sinker is just as useful in saltwater as in fresh for stillfishing or drifting a bait.

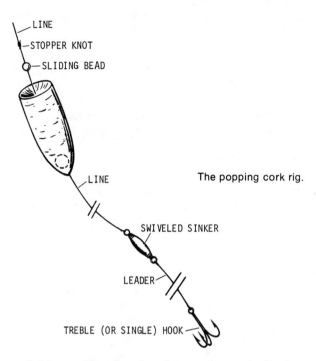

LINE
STOPPER KNOT
SLIDING BEAD

LINE

The popping cork rig.

SWIVELED SINKER

LEADER

TREBLE (OR SINGLE) HOOK

The refinement of this combination, in saltwater just as in freshwater, is to add a sliding float and a stopper, for casting. The arrangement (see details above under "Freshwater Rigs") is exactly the same. One of the most common and productive uses for either the stationary cork or the sliding one is with the popping-cork setup that is used by innumerable anglers after speckled trout (weakfish) over the hundreds of square miles of shallow waters from Florida to Texas. Where the water is about the same depth over a large fishing area, many anglers use a stationary rather than sliding cork. The "popping rods" used are long enough so that casting a rig 2 to 3 feet long is no problem. However, the sliding arrangement is certainly less awkward.

In Part 1, under "Floats," the popping cork and its purpose were briefly mentioned. The float is a long cone shape. Its face—or upper end—is concave. Many of these floats have a small built-in lead weight in the bottom end. The purpose of this is to keep the cork upright and make it revert instantly to an upright position after it is popped. Also, with proper sinker weight below, it rides fairly low to the surface.

Trout or "specks"—as all southern saltwater anglers call the ubiquitous spotted weakfish—feed ravenously on shallow flats, taking mainly grass shrimp but also small fish and other lively forage. They often move in loose groups, and the slurp and roil as each fish grabs a morsel just below surface are easily spotted signs of feeding fish. The popping cork, with its bait—invariably a live shrimp—dangled below, imitates this sound and roil when it is smartly jerked a few inches at a time. Each jerk causes the bait to dance in the water, and the repeated sound and sight draw the fish like magnets.

From the bottom up the rig is as follows. Many popping-cork fishermen favor a treble hook of modest size. It is attached to a leader, usually mono, sometimes wire, of about 18 inches. Between leader and line there is a sinker. A small trolling type with swivels (see Part 1, under "Sinkers") is best, although sometimes clinch sinkers are used. Up the line another foot or more—whatever the feeding depth calls for—is the popping cork, either secured or sliding, with a stopper above. This rig can be used very effectively for other shallow-water fish varieties, too, although it seldom is.

The casting bubble described earlier in this section under "Freshwater Rigs" is not much used in saltwater, although it can be, and is slowly gaining popularity. But small floats for *underwater* (submerged) use (including at times the bubble) are rather common items in several saltwater bottom-fishing rigs. There are three reasons for their use. One of course is to lift a bait a short distance above bottom to keep it from fouling in weeds or rubble, or, if it is alive, to keep it from hiding in bottom debris. The second, and probably most important, reason is that in the surf and in many saltwater situations small bait stealers such as inconsequential nongame catfish and croakers, as well as crabs, are an abominable nuisance. They pick

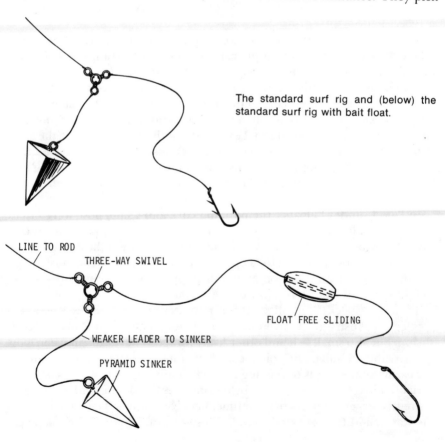

The standard surf rig and (below) the standard surf rig with bait float.

LINE TO ROD

THREE-WAY SWIVEL

FLOAT FREE SLIDING

WEAKER LEADER TO SINKER

PYRAMID SINKER

away at a bait lying on bottom and ruin it before a game fish can find it. The submerged float, held in bounds by a heavy sinker on bottom, lifts the bait well off bottom. The third reason is that this bait, waving easily in current or moving on its own and unable to rest on bottom, is easily seen by desirable species.

Sometimes the small float—generally a slender oval shape—is secured to the bait leader not far from the hook. Sometimes the leader is simply run through the hole down the center of the float, which is allowed to slide on the leader at the whim of the current or the movement of living bait. The bait float is generally employed by casters, and usually in the surf or at least when fishing from a beach. Obviously it can be advantageous also in quiet bay waters where crabs and small fish abound.

Primarily the submerged bait float is a part of either what is called a standard surf rig, or else of the fish-finder rig. The standard surf setup is identical to freshwater bottom rigs that employ a three-way swivel, except that of course heavier line and leader are used, plus hooks of the relevant size, style, and strength. The sinker, however, is almost always a pyramid type. It is tied to a fairly short leader that is attached to one of the swivel rings. The line is secured to another, and the baited-hook leader to the third.

If the bottom may cause hang-ups, most anglers use a leader for the sinker that is of less poundage test than the line or bait leader. Thus if the sinker fouls, it can be broken off by a hard pull and the remainder of the rig saved. Needless to say, the standard surf setup can be used, and is most of the time, without the float.

The fish-finder rig for saltwater is also identical in make-up and idea to that for freshwater (see "Freshwater Rigs"). The line slips through an egg-shaped sinker to allow a bait to roam and a fish to "take" without feeling sinker weight, or it slips through the ring on a heavier and more stabilizing

The famous fish-finder rig. It can be used with an underwater float, but is more often used without one.

pyramid sinker. The current (as in surf) or quietness of the water (as in protected bays) will dictate which sinker design to use. With the heavier and more stable pyramid sinker, and usually in the surf, the bait float is also often a component. Again, however, as with the standard surf rig, the fish finder is undoubtedly more often used without the addition of the submerged float.

There is a minor but ingenious switch that can be tried with the fish finder that employs a float. This is especially productive in surf fishing, particularly when you're "hunting" fish. Too many surf anglers envision all surf-foraging species as grubbing on bottom. That is by no means true. Some are bottom feeders, such as the pompano, but many chase the abundant baitfish in the surf, even right up on top.

To make up this double-level combo, run the line through the eye of the pyramid sinker or the connector attached to it, as mentioned above. Then tie the line to a three-way swivel. To one of the other swivel rings attach a leader of only moderate length with a bottom bait such as squid, cut fish, or mollusk muscle. To the other ring attach a much longer leader that carries another bait popular in the area—a baitfish, sandworm, or shrimp. Eight inches to a foot from this second baited hook, clip on a float.

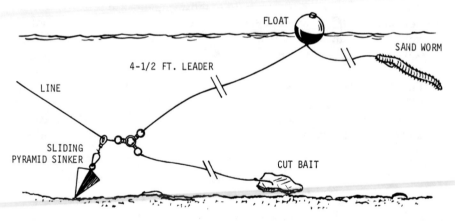

FLOAT

SAND WORM

4-1/2 FT. LEADER

LINE

SLIDING
PYRAMID SINKER

CUT BAIT

The double-level fish-finder surf rig for putting one bait at the surface, another at the bottom.

Cast gently because this rig is a little bit complicated. However, it has the great advantage of showing bait both on bottom and also bouncing up and down right at the top of the surf. Moreover, the line running easily through the sinker connector eye allows both baits to drift or move with currents. This setup can be used also from a boat or pier, as long as the water is not so deep that the bait-float leader becomes unmanageable in length.

There is a most interesting and useful variation of the fish finder that I have never seen used in freshwater but that has found its way here and there along the coasts. According to Joe Bates, in his Outdoor Life book *Fishing,* it supposedly originated in New Jersey, based on the difficulty of casting live baitfish. Cut baits and other dead baits can be cast well enough with the ordinary fish finder and its heavy pyramid sinker. But to cast a live baitfish thus is difficult, without knocking it off the hook or killing it when the big sinker plunks down at the end of a long cast. Thus the ingenious idea was born, for surf and pier and even for close-in boat fishing, of casting the *sinker* and then letting the bait follow down the line.

Here's how it's done. A regular two-way swivel is used, the line attached to one tie, the sinker leader to the other. The sinker leader is usually not long, no more than a foot. The bait leader is somewhat longer, actually whatever the angler desires. The hook is tied directly to it. At the other end is a swivel and snap. The baitfish is hooked so that it will stay alive (see Part 3, under "Minnows"), and the snap is clipped over the tightly slanted line after the cast is made, right at the angler's end. The snap slides down the line. The bait will slide and swim on, and if it seems balky a few modest jerks of the line will hasten it along. The swivel near the pyramid sinker acts as a stopper. By this method an active, fully live bait is presented, rather than a stunned or dead one. And it has freedom to move around all the way down, more so than on the regular fish-finder setup.

Under "Freshwater Rigs" we covered the simple method of casting only the bait, possibly with as light a sinker as possible, if one is needed. There is ample opportunity for this in saltwater too. I remember an afternoon just before sunset when the late Paul Young, of Laredo, Texas, with whom I fished for years, found a big pack of outsize specks for us near an oil installation in a bay near Port Aransas, Texas. We had some giant live bait shrimp that today would never make it as bait because they'd be worth $5 a pound for table fare. These, cast with a reasonably whippy spinning rod, were easy to manipulate. No extra weight was needed.

Rig for sliding a live minnow down the line to avoid injuring it or throwing it off the hook when surfcasting.

The fish were surface-bulging and slurping around near the installation. We anchored off just at easy casting distance and pitched those big, kicking shrimp into the melee. This was a perfect bait presentation. The shrimp, on a free line, darted this way and that. But not far. Trout of 3 to 5 or 6 pounds engulfed each one seconds after it touched water. We simply mopped them up until we ran out of shrimp.

I have fished this way many times, while wading, for channel bass, which in my area are called redfish, using either live shrimp or a peeled shrimp tail. I've used the method with or without a small weight for numerous near-surface marine gamesters, and several of open Gulf waters. It's deadly on kingfish under proper circumstances, on dolphin, blues, and many others. This rig, if indeed it can be called one, is as productive as they come because of its simplicity and spareness.

The sinker-on-end-of-line setups are even more commonly used in saltwater than in fresh. They are identical in concept to the ones described in the freshwater section that utilize the dipsey or some other sinker, the

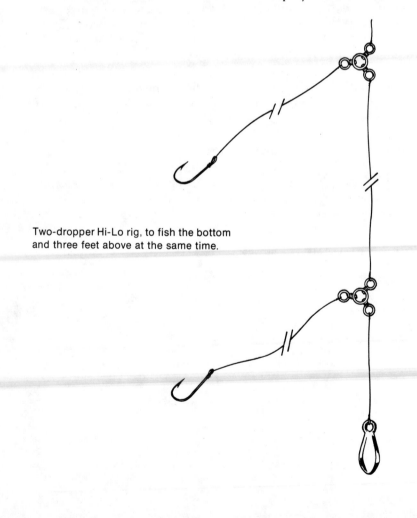

Two-dropper Hi-Lo rig, to fish the bottom and three feet above at the same time.

sinker touching bottom or at least lying at a level where the fish are, and droppers above it carrying the hooks. This is a perfect rig, for example, for saltwater sheepshead because of their exasperatingly light bite. But it is also used for dozens of other saltwater species.

Many, but not all, of the saltwater combinations utilize three-way swivels. One, sometimes known as a Hi-Lo Rig, uses two hook droppers on three-way swivels. The lower one is near bottom, the hook leader much longer than the leader to which the sinker is attached. The other is far enough up the line so that the two hook leaders can't tangle. A bank-type sinker is often used along the East Coast for these. Good-sized dipseys, and heavier pyramids, are also common almost everywhere for this rig. In one form or another these arrangements are used by pier and jetty and surf fishermen, and also by those fishing from boats, either vertically or casting away from the boat or pier.

I have often used, particularly for small saltwater fish, the same setup I described in the freshwater section that has a dipsey on the end of the line and a dropper tied in to the line above it, with no three-way swivel. For quiet water and light tackle, this is perfect for bottom feeders. It is also a

The dipsey-on-end-of-line rig as in freshwater. Good for quiet saltwater or for fishing near pilings.

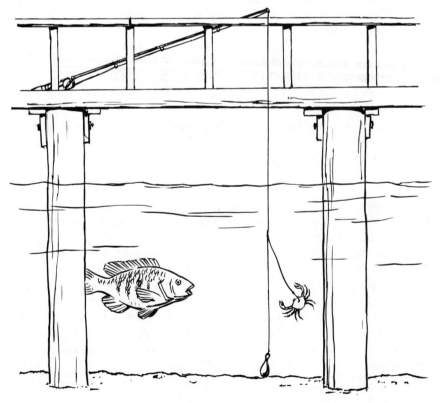

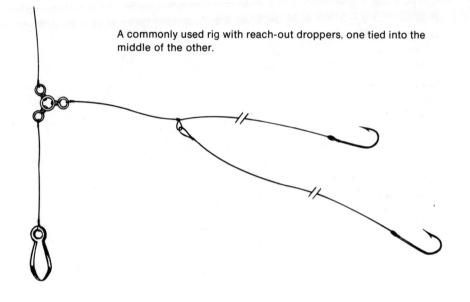

A commonly used rig with reach-out droppers, one tied into the middle of the other.

simple, handy rig, with or without swivel and with one or two hook droppers, for letting down beside a piling on a pier, where fish may hang out but are well up off bottom.

A variation of the combos described above utilizes only *one* hook dropper but *two* hooks. The leaders for each hook are about a foot long. One is tied to a three-way swivel. The other is tied in to that hook leader about halfway along it, with a small snugged-up loop knot. The sinker — bank, dipsey, pyramid, whichever best suits the bottom and current or lack of it — is on a very short leader, no more than 4 inches long. This gets the baits right down on bottom. It is a common setup for flounder and other bottom varieties.

Spreaders are also used in saltwater for bottom fish such as flounder. The idea, as described in the freshwater section, is to make it possible to utilize two hooks at once, mostly right on bottom, and keep them from tangling. In my opinion the spreader is an awkward device, but it has its enthusiasts. In saltwater use it is seldom suspended, but a bank or other good holding sinker is used on a short tie that keeps the entire rig on bottom.

One possibility with sinkers, especially for saltwater where by and large fish are not as shy of complicated rigs as in freshwater, is to attach a snap to the sinker leader in all rigs using a three-way swivel or any other where the sinker is at line's end. The reason for doing this, in the surf or for general bottom fishing, is that you cannot always tell how much weight you are going to need for a particular situation. You may find you need more than you anticipated. This entails snipping off a tied-on sinker and retying for a new, larger size. If several changes must be made, your sinker leader will be progressively shortened, and the process is also time-consuming. A snap, or one of the connectors with a sliding collar that usually works more easily, makes a quick change possible.

Without doubt many saltwater bait rigs other than those described might be dredged up by searching diligently along the Atlantic, Gulf, and Pacific coasts. I remember years back seeing a salty old gentleman at Morro Bay, California, for example, who carried a bundle of sections of welding rod in a kind of quiver he'd made for them. To either end of each was brazed a tie eye. Each rod was about a yard long. He tied his stout line to one end and attached a heavy, short-shanked hook directly to the other end by a split ring.

He baited with a chunk of fish and pitched this unusual device in a kind of tossed-out cast right among the jumble of submerged rocks. The metal rod slid down among the crevices. Rock piles like that are home to a dozen or more species of Pacific rockfish and other hiding quarry. Presently he had a bite. He set the hook quickly. The fish tried stubbornly to retreat into its lair somewhere deep in the maze. But the stiff rod would not allow this. It couldn't be pulled around corners, and usually could move little deeper than where it had originally lodged. The angler unceremoniously hauled forth his prize. Now and then a rod stuck and he had to break off. He simply replaced his unique rig and continued.

It would be impossible to ferret out all such unique devices and arrangements. But the basic ones given here are the standards used for many years over a wide territory. They have proved themselves productive. Your own alterations may devise new ones that are more so, but the ones I've given are the ones with which to begin.

The spreader as used in saltwater for bottom fish often has the hook droppers longer than the one for the sinker. This is sometimes called a "flounder rig" but is useful for any bottom-feeding species.

PART 3

Freshwater Baits and How to Fish Them

"NATURAL" BAITS MIGHT BE broadly defined as those that occur in nature, but our focus here must be somewhat narrower. The baits with which we are concerned are living creatures such as minnows, worms, and insects, or the same creatures fresh-dead, or sometimes frozen for storage. Certainly there are other baits. Trout anglers nowadays in some areas use canned kernel corn, cheese, even marshmallows as bait, and successfully. Dough baits and prepared stink baits for catfish are other concoctions that catch fish. But they are not what might be called "natural" baits, and so they will not be included here.

I suppose almost any item an angler can think of might somehow tempt a fish to hit. I once sat tossing dandelion buds into a hole where rock bass lay. The fish would dart out, seize one and then spit it out. A hook on one would have caught fish. I've watched bass and bluegills smack dropping fruit such as mulberries that overhung a lake or stream. The same fish will snap sometimes at tiny twigs pitched to them. But the reason for those hits and the others mentioned is simply the motion of the item.

So probably one legitimate definition of a natural bait might be a living or fresh-dead creature that is taken as food to be swallowed and not simply struck on impulse because it moves. Most of these natural baits occur in the environment of the fish. They are creatures upon which the fish habitually forage, and they are therefore recognized as legitimate food and so are readily ingested.

However, there are notable exceptions. Perhaps the most striking is the angleworm. In some slow trout streams that flow through boggy places it is true that worms often wash out into the current from the banks. I remember catching brook trout that were stuffed with worms after a flooding rise on the Black River in northern Michigan. Yet this too is an exception. Most fish that eagerly bite on worms probably live out their lives generation after generation without ever seeing or tasting one unless it is offered on a hook. Probably the combination of appearance, wiggle if any, smell possibly, and taste indicates to a worm-eating fish that this is proper food. In addition there are various aquatic worms that are eaten rather commonly. So the angleworm, for whatever reason, is a classic and most productive freshwater bait.

Its larger relative, the night crawler, is as everyone knows a killer offering. I've never found a satisfactory explanation of the exact reason. Presumably fish see few night crawlers, if any. They do eat eels and aquatic salamanders and very occasionally small snakes. Perhaps there is a resemblance. Or it may be that the look of that big, soft, juicy, undulating critter is simply irresistible.

One of the most interesting perplexities about the appeal of night crawlers is that the walleye, with a diet in most instances about 90 percent made up of small forage fish, eagerly seizes them. The June Bug spinner trailing a big night crawler has been a northern walleye rig par excellence for many years. Walleye guides on some of the lakes use a lure such as a Flatfish that wriggles fast even when trolled slowly, and they add a hunk of night crawler on either side to the trebles that in most Flatfish models are set on a horizontal wire. The lure with crawler commonly produces four times as much as the lure alone.

Regardless of these exceptions, a bait fisherman can never go wrong checking the forage of greatest abundance in the water where he'll be fishing, and then using for bait something native to that lake or stream, something its fish commonly feed on. It is obvious that a fish will take most readily what it is used to eating, and this is what is most readily available in that particular habitat. In some waters the choice of forage is not broad. A bass in a lake loaded with shiners may take one of those before it would bother with a strange-looking crayfish, of which let's presume the same lake has none. The reverse may occur in a lake with few minnows but teeming with crayfish.

All this is just basic. Using the obvious bait is a quick means to a successful end. It does not mean that you should avoid trying other baits. I recall one time simply loading up on yellow perch using leeches for bait. This was in a Great Lakes bay where I'm positive the diet was mostly small minnows. Leeches I'd guess were few, if present at all. Yet for some reason the perch really went for them. Experiments of this kind will often reveal a "secret" for filling a stringer when other standard approaches fail.

There is, however, one important consideration. Any accomplished bait fisherman must have a fair understanding of what the various fish species eat, that is, whether they are selective or ready to eat almost anything. As I mentioned, the walleye is ordinarily a heavy feeder upon small fish. Certainly it will take other food, but some kinds of bait it would be most unlikely to try. I won't say, for example, that a walleye can't be caught on a big grasshopper, but I will say that if I was going walleye fishing, grasshoppers for bait would not be the first enticement I'd think of.

Each freshwater game fish is addicted to particular items of diet as its main course or courses, when those are available. For example, it is most interesting that among the several sunfishes some feed almost entirely on insects, varied worms, and small crustaceans, while at least one or two grab small minnows in preference, even though they will accept insect baits. At the end of this section on freshwater baits I have arranged a chart that lists the various freshwater fish species and opposite each the baits most avidly taken. This should give you a handy, quick reference and some clues as to the basic forage of each species. But again, experiments are never amiss.

Baits for freshwater include small forage fishes, and some larger ones, such as good-sized suckers eaten by pike and muskellunge. Fish spawn — salmon eggs chiefly — must also be included. Angleworms and night crawlers are of course standard. Some of the amphibians — frogs and salamanders — are prime freshwater baits. Among the crustaceans the crayfish is the most important freshwater tidbit. Some mollusks are also eaten by fish equipped to crush them, such as freshwater drum and redear sunfish, and meat from opened mollusks makes a fine bait in some situations.

Numerous insects are among the most important of freshwater baits. This should be noted well by the marine angler new to freshwater. Saltwater fish seldom have any opportunity to feed on insects, but freshwater varieties in almost any latitude or type of water are constantly in the presence of insects. In their various forms insects furnish a most substantial portion of the diet of numerous freshwater species. They may be eaten as mature insects, as larvae — caterpillars and grubs — or as aquatic nymphs living on bottom in lakes and streams. All of these are the mainstay baits used by freshwater anglers to fill stringers and skillets.

Minnows

Although the term is not used quite as commonly nowadays, in the past when a fisherman spoke of using live bait, others assumed he meant minnows. In freshwater fishing all small forage fish are usually lumped together and called "minnows." This is logical, because most of the common forage fish used as baits belong to the minnow family, *Cyprinidae*. The family is large, but most of its members are small or of only modest size. All of the various species of shiners, chubs, and daces belong to this family, and these are among the best known of bait minnows.

The goldfish is also a member of the minnow family. Goldfish minnows are often used for crappies and other fish. So are fingerling carp, another minnow-family member. In some waters, however, goldfish or carp minnows are prohibited. The possibility of them monopolizing the lake if any

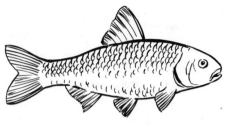

COMMON SHINER

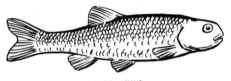

CREEK CHUB

Common varieties of bait minnows (from top): common shiner; creek chub; greased chub.

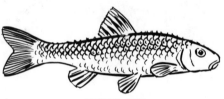

GREASED CHUB

should go free alive is a danger to fisheries management. In certain waters in a few states all minnow fishing is prohibited. Thus it is mandatory to check the laws and know what waters are legally open to minnow fishing, and what varieties of minnows, if any, may be prohibited.

Sucker "minnows" are also much used as bait. The popular use of the term minnow with the sucker seems logical, but it is not actually a member of the minnow family. It is in a large family of its own, the *Catostomidae*. Sometimes small sunfishes are used for bait, and of course they too would be lumped in with minnows. Throughout the South, in scores of impoundments where the gizzard and threadfin shad are mainstays of game-fish forage, young of these species are extremely important as "minnow" baits. In fact, any freshwater baitfish so used locally and for specialized purposes might be classified colloquially under "minnows," or the method "fishing with minnows." Bass, most panfish, walleyes, perch, pike, trout, and catfish all feed on small fishes and thus readily succumb to a minnow tethered to hook and line because it appears to be easy prey.

As indicated earlier, it is useful to know at least roughly the importance of minnows in the diet of the various game fishes. As an example, in a lake of modest size that I built with a dam on a stretch of creek we own, there are five different varieties of sunfish. Out of curiosity I made a study of

61

COMMON SUCKER

CHUB SUCKER

GIZZARD SHAD

Other popular baitfish (from top): common sucker; young of various suckers are used as minnows, and for some fishing suckers 6 to 12 inches long are needed. Chubsucker; this is a stand-in for the sucker in some locations. The gizzard shad, a bait much used across the south.

which ones took which baits (or their artificial imitations) most readily. The bluegills would occasionally accept a small minnow, but minnows certainly were not a prime item of diet. They took worms or insects far more eagerly. Redear sunfish, or shellcrackers, seldom were enthused over minnows. Worms were their dish. When I put on a small minnow, invariably the first sunfish I caught was a yellowbreast. They avidly seized this bait. This sunfish, extremely popular in the Southeast, of course will take other baits, but of the true sunfishes it is the one to which minnows are an important item of diet.

There is no reason to use anything but minnows for crappies. In fact, this is such a standard bait for them that in many parts of the country fishermen speak of "crappie minnows," meaning minnows about 1½ to 2 inches long. Crappies will take minnows all year but are most easily caught during the spring when huge concentrations gather along lakeshores, particularly among small bushes, for spawning. All you have to do is drop a minnow down into a bush top under water and *whammo!*

A friend of mine in Wisconsin once built a private fishing dock on a lake he owned, designed especially to entice crappies. I fished there often. The walkway was a rectangle along the shore, over water 5 to 10 feet deep. Beneath the broad walkway he sank a tangle of cut brush. This drew scads of minnows to its cover, and the forage drew scads of crappies. Heated, cov-

BROOK SILVERSIDES

MUD MINNOW

Bait dealers sell a variety of minnows, some not native. Here are examples of native species often used for fish such as crappies, white bass, yellow perch.

TOP MINNOW

BULLHEAD MINNOW

ered winter-fishing docks, popular especially in Oklahoma, do the same thing. We just dropped minnows down over the rail, using a small float and a split shot, which placed them within a few inches of the cover, and in no time we had a big string of crappies.

There is no reason to use anything but minnows, of the crappie-minnow size, for yellow perch. Certainly perch take worms and some other baits, but in most waters they are predominantly minnow feeders. The pleasant slant on minnow fishing for perch is that, while most other species insist that the bait be alive and kicking, often yellow perch don't care. They'll take fresh-dead ones when hungry just as quickly.

Years ago I used to fish each spring on Lake Huron's Saginaw Bay when yellow perch swarmed inshore on their spring spawning run. A friend taught me how to preserve minnows in salt. It's a simple procedure: a layer of rock salt in the bottom of a big earthen crock, a layer of fresh minnows, and so on. Store the crock in a cool place. They become tough and will keep for weeks. I'd carry a batch in a shirt pocket, to avoid the bother of fiddling with live minnows. The salt in them actually appeals to the perch, and after one is in the water a bit it begins to soften up. Seldom was one dunked without a bite long enough to get very soft!

About 90 percent of the diet of the perch's big relative, the walleye, is made up of minnows, which in this case should be somewhat larger. Three inches is a good size. You don't want them too big, or the walleye mouths the bait. It's better to have one grab the minnow all in one gulp. There are of course many ways to fish minnows for walleyes. Some anglers rig them to troll deep and very slowly. Some of the best minnow fishing I ever devised for walleyes was done with a bobber and small sinker, and the minnow only a couple of feet below.

On a good lake we would look for an island, or an "almost" island—a small underwater hill that came within a foot or so of surface. I recall one of these, in Wisconsin, that had floating aquatic weeds atop it. Walleyes, as some anglers may know, usually make at least two feeding migrations a day, early morning and late afternoon, from deep water to upper areas attractive to minnows. The cone of that submerged hill was rocky, and the cover up top was a solid flurry of baitfish. We'd anchor a boat within casting distance, toss minnow and bobber near the vegetation. The result was stacks of superb fillets on the table. Bobber fishing of that sort is great fun.

White bass, yellow bass, and white perch all take minnows readily. For these fish the crappie-minnow size is perfect, and usually the bait produces best when stillfished where schools will find it.

There are a good many black-bass fishermen who never use anything except live minnows. Bass are not eager to accept a dead one, but lively ones they can't resist. There is broad divergence in the size of minnows used for bass in various parts of the country, and in the riggings used. Most bass minnows average 2 to 4 inches. Some years ago in Florida I learned from a

Minnows fished near underwater knolls are deadly on walleyes during daily upward feeding migrations.

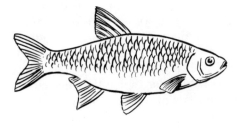

The golden shiner, abundant in the south, is a superb big-bass bait. Try specimens a foot long fished below a big bobber along hyacinth beds.

guide to use huge shiners—literally a foot long—and plop one with no sinker on the line up against the edges of a water-hyacinth bed. A big bobber completed the rig, 2 or 3 feet above the bait.

Some of the biggest shiners could pull the bobber down but couldn't keep it there. When it went down and streaked off under the floating vegetation I knew a bass had it—a BIG bass. We'd let out line until the bass stopped, then gently snug up and ram the hook home. It was quite common to take bass of 6 to 9 pounds or more this way.

Among the most perfect fish, all round, for minnow fishing are pike and pickerel. Minnows should be of substantial size. They can be fished, alive, along weed beds beneath a bobber. Or, fresh-dead minnows can be rigged for trolling or casting.

Now a brief look at rigs for minnow fishing. Bits of this information have been scattered over previous pages, but for easy and more concentrated reference, the following comments should be helpful. In the section about freshwater rigs, several were described that are perfect for fishing minnows. Regardless of the fish species, stillfishing with live minnows, with a float, is one of the most effective methods. Simply toss out the float and sinker with a minnow-baited hook and let it stay there. Or, cast it out and move it a bit every few minutes, or else retrieve very slowly.

In casting live minnows, however, you have to be gentle. Otherwise you kill or cast off the bait. Where possible, drifting a minnow below a float is extremely productive. Floating a stream and letting one ride the current, guiding it as needed, or simply drifting in a breeze along the shoreline of a lake presents the lively bait over much area, and at its best.

The rig I described with a dipsey sinker on bottom and one or two droppers on the line above, either using a three-way swivel or simply tying in the droppers, is a fine minnow-fishing method. But you have to select the right type of bottom so that the live minnow does not get into weeds and hide, or at least have the dropper high enough to avoid that. Where there are short bottom weeds, occasionally one can rig with a submerged bubble as described under "Freshwater Rigs." This keeps the minnow up off bottom. Always try to fish a live minnow so it is a short distance away from weeds or other cover. It will constantly attempt to gain cover, and that movement will alert game fish.

Under proper conditions, using light tackle, a live minnow can be cast with only a small split shot to force it down. Otherwise it will often attempt to surface. The angler must control the minnow, keeping it from hiding. But as it swims naturally—even perhaps without a sinker of any kind if the minnow is large enough to cast and weed beds are nearby—any game fish is certain to consider it easy pickings. The fish-finder rig has the same effect. The only problem with the fish-finder or slip-sinker setup for live-minnow fishing is that the bait may successfully bury itself in nearby cover. But if it is fished near, but not in, cover, and the line held barely snug, the minnow can wander, and when a fish takes it there is no pressure on the line.

Every live-minnow fisherman has his favorite way of hooking the bait. The hooking theory is simple enough: do the least possible damage to the bait, so that it will stay alive as long as possible. It is important to handle minnows carefully while getting them out of the bait bucket and placing them on the hook. Small ones especially if squeezed hard will quickly succumb.

There are three basic ways of placing a live minnow on a hook: hooking it through both lips (never through only one); hooking it in the tail; hooking it under or just ahead of the dorsal fin, but above the backbone. The consensus seems to be that the dorsal hook placement is best for lively minnow action. However, great care must be taken not to thrust the hook into any vital organs but only through the flesh. Never use hooks larger or heavier than needed for the fish you're after. Large or heavy-shanked hooks do much damage to minnows. Occasionally large minnows are hooked with a double-hook rig. One goes through both lips. This is the

Three basic ways of putting minnows on hook are: hooking through both lips, in the tail, or under or ahead of the dorsal fin.

hook that actually holds the minnow and takes the pull on the line. A second hook is passed back on a short piece of monofil tied to the first hook and is embedded in the tail.

Fishing dead minnows is somewhat different. As I've noted, some freshwater fish will accept them even when they are stillfished. Some won't. Most

Occasionally large minnows are hooked with a double-hook rig.

anglers fish either fresh-dead or frozen baitfish they've kept in a freezer, or purchased frozen at a bait store, by rigging them to be cast or trolled. The movement of course simulates a live, possibly crippled, minnow, and the movement is what appeals to the fish.

Most anglers who cast minnows like to have them run straight, as if they are alive. Sometimes this is accomplished by simply hooking the minnow as if it were alive, through both lips, as a rule from the bottom upward. But minnows either dead or alive are easily cast off the hook when impaled thus unless the fisherman is very gentle and an expert caster. On occasion dead minnows are trolled this same way. A striking fish, however, can jerk the bait off without getting the hook.

One of the recognized best methods of hooking, or rigging, a minnow for casting is to run hook and line through the mouth and out one gill. Then pull just enough line through so that you can form a simple loop, or hitch. This goes around the minnow ahead of the dorsal fin. But before you snug it down, embed the hook in the side of the fish back toward the tail, with the hook point outward so that it will set easily. Then pull the line and loop without bending the tail of the minnow. When the loop is tight, the minnow will lie straight on the hook. Trussed thus, a baitfish can be cast many times without harming it.

A good method of hooking dead minnows for casting: pass hook and line through mouth and out gill; make loop around body; embed hook in side near tail.

It can also be trolled this way. But generally other rigs are used for trolling. One of these is so designed that the baitfish will turn slowly. The hook is thrust downward through the lower lip and pulled clear through, with some line or leader following. Leaving a bit of loose line, the hook is then brought up and thrust clear down through the head from the top, behind the eyes. The entire hook and some trailing line are pulled through. The hook is then embedded barb out, through the side of the bait well back toward the tail. Now the line from in front of the minnow is slowly and gently snugged up. The tail of the bait is held just slightly bent. This will cause it to turn when trolled (or cast). Note that this method of hooking through the head makes a loop that pulls tight at the snout. Thus rigged, a

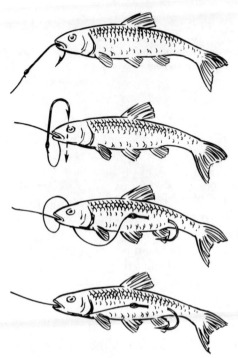

Rigged as shown, dead minnow will turn slowly when cast or trolled.

minnow is well secured to stay just as you want it. More or less bend (and turning rate) in the bait can be had by adjustment of the rigging.

The earlier section covering hooks described the several varieties of hooks with a pin and other fastener added for securing dead minnows. That material may be consulted for further ideas about specialized minnow riggings. Also, many minnow fishermen carry in their tackle several large sewing needles of various sizes to facilitate passing a line properly through the minnow. With the line threaded to the needle, it is easy to pass it as desired through the minnow and *then* tie the hook in place. This method is fast and minimizes bait damage.

Large sewing needle expedites job of running line down through middle of a dead minnow.

If you intend literally to "sew" a minnow on a hook by several wraps of line around and through its body, the needle is mandatory. And in such cases the point should be thrust through first. However, a variant used by some is to push the needle point first into a small, round stick or piece of doweling. The eye, thus left to hold the line, is then thrust through to truss the bait properly. There are disadvantages to this method. On small bait-fish the eye used instead of the point may do too much damage. In addition, regular sewing needles may not be long enough for large minnows. Occasionally you may find in a tackle store a ready-made gadget with a longer shank and wood handle.

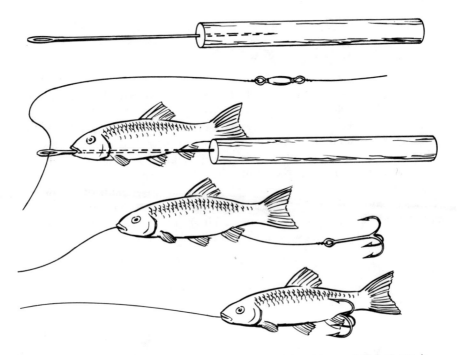

A switch on the previous method. Needle point is thrust into small dowel, eye is used for threading line and for penetration. This is only used with large minnows.

There are many ways to attach dead minnows. The accompanying draw-ings should be helpful and perhaps spark ideas of your own. When trolling minnows, particularly those rigged so that they will turn, it is necessary to utilize swivels to avoid line twist. In fact, for either casting or trolling most anglers use one of the trolling sinkers, of proper size, described under "Equipment." These are available in many forms—with a swivel at one end

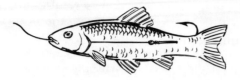

Three more ways of attaching dead minnows.

and a snap at the other, with swivels at either end, with bead chain, with swivels and a keel, and so on.

Sometimes a minnow is trussed so that a treble hook is embedded at the vent. The best such rigs—and in fact any cast or trolled minnow rigs—are often made much more effective by using a spinner a short distance above the minnow. The flash of the spinner is a provocative attractor. This is the principle that has made the forbiddingly awkward "chain of cowbells"— strings of spinners diminishing in size—so effective for trolling. The multiple flash alerts fish from a distance. The minnow (or other bait) is there when the fish moves close to investigate.

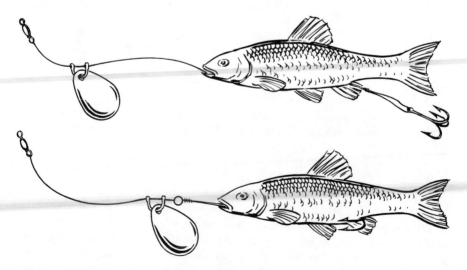

Treble hook and spinner rig for casting and trolling dead minnows.

The ways to fish minnows are as varied as the ways of attaching them or rigging them. Walleye fishermen often drift, letting a live minnow with a sinker ahead of it (but no float) down onto a bar. They raise the rod tip every few seconds to lift and drop back the bait. Stream fishing with minnows, particularly for trout, is much overlooked. It can be deadly. Trout certainly go after live minnows, but they also grab dead ones—especially fresh-dead specimens—that tumble naturally. Because current and rocks may strip off a bait simply hooked through the lips, a good method is to use the rigging I described for casting—passing the hook and line through the mouth, out one gill, making a snug loop around the body ahead of the dorsal and embedding the hook in the side near the tail. This rig should be cast either with no sinker or the very lightest one possible—a single small split shot a few inches to a foot ahead of the bait. Make your casts upstream and across. Let the minnow tumble naturally but keep the rod tip up and retrieve line at current speed. Strike immediately if the minnow hesitates.

Comparatively few fishermen nowadays gather their own minnows. They buy them from bait shops or minnow farms. Always try to obtain minnows for live-minnow fishing that are tough. Numerous minnow farms nowadays raise varieties and strains that are long-lived when on the hook. When possible, also use tough-fleshed minnows for casting and trolling. They hold together longer, and you don't have to change baits so often.

Suckers for Muskies

Using big whole suckers for muskellunge fishing is a specialized kind of "minnow" fishing, since it uses an already big fish to catch a bigger fish. Those who practice this art use suckers of at least a pound in weight, which means they are ordinarily 14 or 15 inches long.

The sucker is one of the most common rough fish in most muskie waters, and it is a prime item of forage for the muskellunge. Adult muskies seldom take small baits, or small food portions. They smash a big sucker to stun it, then move back in to seize it, turn it and swallow it headfirst, taking their time. It may not be legal (state laws should be checked) in all muskie waters to fish live suckers for muskies. But where it is, this method is far more productive than casting artificials.

The procedure is quite simple. Most experts hook the sucker through both tough lips. Muskies ordinarily slash at a forage fish from the side, or above, and crosswise, then pick it up with the tip of the snout, not grabbing with the whole maw. They then carry it to their lair or at least some distance from strike point before turning it to swallow it. If the hook is under the dorsal, the fish will feel it. They are very whimsical and wary, and usually drop the bait if the hook is immediately felt.

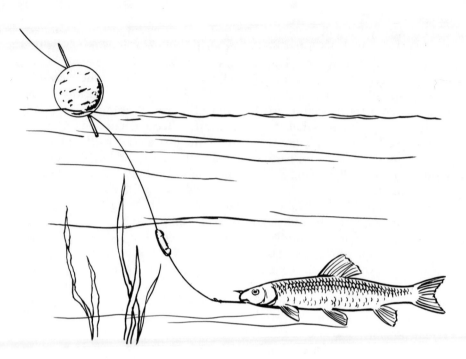

Typical simple setup for fishing muskellunge with foot-long live sucker.

A large bobber is used and the sucker turned loose in a channel or along a shoreline with suitable-looking submerged debris. When a fish takes, the bobber goes under and moves away. The boat follows, using oars, never a motor, and the angler pays out line, keeping snugged up but with no pressure whatever on the line. There is no way except a sixth sense and luck to tell when to finally strike. Usually the fish stops, often lying on bottom for a long period holding the bait. As it moves again, most of the time the sucker has been partially or wholly swallowed, and the hook can be set.

I fished this way one year in northern Wisconsin after spending several days with a bevy of guides who were trying rather desperately to help get a big muskie for me for a series of pictures for a magazine assignment I was doing. All of us cast artificials literally thousands of times. Fish followed occasionally, in that exasperating way of the muskie. But over several days not one strike did we get. Totally frustrated, we finally tried fishing a big sucker on a private lake of about 600 acres that was loaded with muskellunge. In an hour we had a fine specimen. Fortunately, it did not have the big sucker far down and was hooked only in the jaw. We were able to gaff it through the lower lip and release it with no more than superficial wounds.

During this fishing I listened to endless tales from the guides about their experiences. One old gentleman who'd been at it many years described for me how he worked hard for a client and rowed him endless miles, dragging a big live sucker. Finally they had a "take." The muskie moved off ever so slowly. The guides quietly rowed the boat to keep up. The fish just as slowly took them almost half a mile across to the slope of an island. There it immediately dropped the bait! The bobber came to surface. The sucker was badly slashed, but the big brute had made no attempt to swallow it. Such are the exasperating habits of the muskellunge. Nonetheless, live-sucker fishing for muskellunge is often far more productive than casting artificials.

A much more sporting method than fishing a live sucker is casting a dead one. This is a high art, filled with drama. Years ago I learned about how it is done, also from guides in northern Wisconsin who were experts at it. One of them detailed the rigging process step by step for me. Probably it differs among enthusiasts of this exacting method. He had brought a few live suckers of a pound each in a live box. He hauled one out and whacked it on the head with pliers to kill it. He used stout woven fishline for his rig. The tying process is tricky and requires practice. The bait is to be cast, often hour after hour, without tearing apart. It must strike just right on the water and move on the retrieve naturally, as if swimming.

The piece of stout woven line used for the rigging was a separate one, not attached to hook or reel. One loop went around the body behind the pectoral fins. Another passed around behind the gills. These were harnessed together on the lower (belly) side of the fish, by a lengthwise double strand, and the loop of that harness was passed through the flesh of the chin from below and out the mouth no more than an inch. Another loop was then tied just behind the heavy lips and pulled tight. The big, stout-shanked hook at line's end was not put into the sucker at all. The harness loop coming out the mouth was tied to the bend of the hook. Thus the hook was right at the end of the sucker's snout.

Casting such a bait is hard physical work. Most experts cast it in a high arc with a stiff, two-handed muskie rod. It comes down with a resounding splat. It must then instantly be reeled in at top speed, since a slow retrieve allows a muskie to spy out the ruse. On my first experience as an observer I saw a big muskie come ripping along the surface as the sucker hit, pursue it with furious speed and slash it viciously. The fisherman then let off slack to let the bait fall back, simulating death, and waited.

I recall asking another native in the boat with us how long the wait would be. By now the muskie had picked up the bait and moved off with it, then stopped. These erratic fish may lie on bottom holding the sucker for ten minutes, half an hour, or longer. The suspense is high. After holding the bait a long time, the fish may drop it and leave. Finally this one started to swim away. This usually — but not always — means the fish has turned the bait around and taken it wholly into its mouth, or swallowed it.

Presently, as we followed quietly in the boat, the fish stopped again. Then it moved once more. The angler made his gamble. He struck powerfully. The line snugged, the water blew up, and the big fellow erupted from it. The muskie was solidly hooked. When casting suckers in this manner, it takes much practice to place the bait properly in likely spots and handle it efficiently. But all in all this is one of the most dramatic of all bait-fishing endeavors, and a highly productive one.

Cut Bait

The term "cut bait" is more common among saltwater than freshwater anglers. In general it means a piece of fish. There are refinements, dealing with how the bait is cut—i.e., in a chunk ("cut bait" in a more restricted sense) or a lengthwise strip ("strip bait"). But as used here in this freshwater section the term will encompass any piece of fish used as bait.

Not all inland game fish will readily accept cut bait. Very occasionally bass will tentatively take a fresh chunk, but this is an exception. None of the sunfishes and crappies are eager for it, although yellow perch can be caught on parts of small minnows now and then when you run short of other bait.

As stated earlier, pike and pickerel generally like live minnows, but there is also an excellent rig for pike casting that utilizes a chunk of fish, usually sucker meat. Either a spoon, such as a standard wobbler, or else a large spinner is used. When using a large spinner, which trails a treble hook, simply impale a strip of sucker meat. It can be placed on only one of the hooks, so that it trails back, or wrapped around and impaled on all three.

The action of a wobbling spoon is inhibited by doing this, but some anglers use a short length of wire spliced in between the treble and the rear

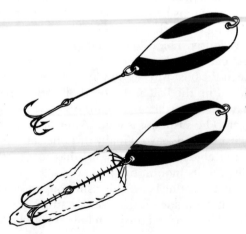

Pike and lake trout setup using wire extension behind spoon, to which a sucker strip is secured with a thread.

split ring of the spoon. The strip of sucker about 1½ inches long is then stitched with thread, the broad end at the rear of the spoon and the thread running several times through the split ring. More thread stitched through the meat holds it to the wire, and the narrow tail protrudes a bit behind the hook. Although this rig is productive, it is a lot of bother.

The idea of using sucker meat behind spinner or spoon is that fish are attracted by the flash of the metal blade and then smell the sucker meat. Fish that won't hit the artificials are "suckers" for this setup. It is also used most successfully for lake trout, which are extremely indiscriminate feeders. I have caught scads of them in Canada by baiting a hook with a chunk of sucker, clinching on the sinker or else using a dipsey and dropper rig, and fishing right on bottom. This works particularly well in spring when the trout swarm over fairly shallow inshore shoals shortly after the ice goes out.

One year while I was fishing Gullwing Lake in Ontario my guide carried packages of sucker meat with the skin on that he had kept frozen. We'd cut a small strip and impale it on all three hooks of a treble behind a large spinner. Leaving the skin on made the bait very tough. It stayed on the hook well and could not easily be stripped off by a short strike. We trolled with this rig. It was deadly. We watched other anglers trolling spinners alone and doing almost nothing, while we took limits.

Strip of sucker meat wrapped on treble hook of spinner is great setup for lake trout.

Although cut bait is seldom used for the other trouts, it will catch any of them. Numerous fishermen do not realize this, and I had fished for years before I did. I was fishing a prime brook-trout stream at the time, using dry flies. I was doing all right, casting and moving upstream. The size limit was 7 inches. I had creeled possibly a half dozen, nothing over 8 or 9 inches. But they are fine eating, and I was happy. I really didn't expect large brookies from this stream anyway.

Then I met a native lad working downstream. He had a hopelessly awkward batch of worn tackle: an ancient fly rod to which he had attached a dilapidated baitcasting reel filled with old-fashioned woven black line. No leader. The hook tied directly to the line. It was impossible, I knew, to catch a wary brookie that way in this crystal water. But the boy was trailing something on a stringer, and when I got close my eyes popped. He had three trout that easily weighed 2 pounds each.

When I asked how he'd got them, he reached in his shirt pocket and pulled out a chub that had probably been 4 inches long but was now half that. He explained that he first fished a small, near-stagnant pond, an offshoot from the stream, with a tiny hook and a bit of worm. When he had

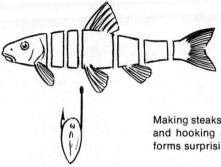

Making steaks out of small baitfish such as a chub, and hooking across through skin on both sides, forms surprisingly good bait for trout.

caught several chubs, he went fishing. With a pocketknife he cut a cross-section chunk of fresh chub, put it on his trout hook and drifted it down into the holes and under logs.

"You catch the little ones on worms and stuff," he said, "but my dad has been catching big ones like this ever since I can remember. He taught me."

Later I tried this method. The results were nearly unbelievable. I also caught many browns that way. Rainbows don't seem as eager, but they can be taken thus.

There is an effective trick little used by, and possibly not even known to, most bait fishermen, and that is the use of what is called the "throat latch" cut from a caught fish. I first learned of this when fishing for yellow bass one time in Iowa. I caught the first one on a small spoon. But artificials didn't do well that day. A nearby fisherman told me to cut out the piece of tough flesh and white skin of the throat, that portion lying between the gills and ahead of the pectoral fins.

I placed this as directed on a hook, using a dipsey sinker and a dropper above it, and tossed it out. I literally caught a bucketful of yellow bass on that one throat latch from one of their buddies, crawling it slowly along.

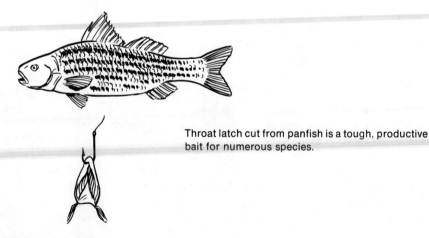

Throat latch cut from panfish is a tough, productive bait for numerous species.

This will work also on white bass, white perch, and lake trout. One time in western Montana, on a lake that contains unbelievably large yellow perch, I used this gimmick. Actually we were after big cutthroat trout with lures but weren't getting any. I learned of the presence of the big perch, happened to hook a very small kokanee on a trout spoon, cut out the throat latch and fished it on bottom for perch. It worked like a charm.

Whitefish and ciscoes can often be caught on tiny bits of cut bait fished down on bottom in their haunts, on a very small hook. Catfish eagerly gobble cut bait, and so do freshwater drum. Several years ago I fished with the Burnham brothers of Marble Falls, Texas. They are famous for their predator calls and calling ability, but they are also expert fishermen. There had been a rise on the Texas Colorado River, which flows through Marble Falls. They called and said this was the time to catch a boatload of modest-sized blue cats, which are excellent eating.

They brought for bait a big package of young gizzard shad that had been frozen. The shad were possibly 3 inches in average length. We pinched or cut these small shad in half and baited with them. Gizzard shad are smelly, strong fish. The juice oozing from these chunks served as a veritable magnet. We fished right on bottom and caught both blue cats and drum.

Gizzard shad three inches long, cut or pinched in two so strong juices flow, works wonders with species such as catfish and drum.

Almost any fish that feeds on other fish can be caught with a piece of fish. Certainly some are more avid than others. But to paraphrase the old adage about bread, half a fish is better than none — and often a single slice gets better results than a whole living baitfish.

Worms and Night Crawlers

It is a high compliment to the effectiveness of worms that a majority of freshwater fishermen equate the term bait with worms. Anyone who is bait fishing is envisioned as using worms, unless he states otherwise. The so-called "garden hackle" has been lauded since early fishing history as perhaps the most effective seducer of the greatest variety of freshwater fish. Among all the game and eating fish from inland waters, some species take worms more eagerly than others, yet it is doubtful if there are any that at one time or another are not caught on this lowly offering.

The so-called night crawler is of course just an oversize variety of angleworm. There are hundreds of species in the family, long, short, fat, skinny, bright reddish to dark earth color. Although worm fishing is thought of as a lowly sport, I still recall with excitement the ritual of worm digging when I was a kid. Today there are long treatises about how to gather worms, how to prepare them for fishing by "scouring" them for hours or days in sand or leaf mold, how to raise and keep them. We did things much more simply, and we caught lots of fish.

We went out behind the barn, or to some spot where the earth was moist but not wet, and soft. The shovel cut into it, bare feet kicked the clods apart, and we pounced on the wiggling worms, popping them into a tin can with a bit of earth in it. The drama of discovering a patch of dirt laced with fat worms was part of the total fishing enjoyment. Then off to the nearby slow, meandering river, our bare feet plopping in the thick dust of a country road, where horses and buggies or teams and wagons pulverized it but a motor vehicle was a rarity.

I don't recall anyone teaching me how to put a worm on a hook. You just got hold of the protesting, slippery critter and threaded it on. We did find out that a gob dripping from a hook was best for catfish and that a worm threaded from the center toward the thick end so that the other end wiggled amply was irresistible to sunfish and bass in the oxbow stream. Some old-timers just threaded a little bit of the thick end on, letting the rest hang off.

Then, as I described in the beginning of this book, with a stove-bolt nut for a sinker and a bottle cork or a piece of whittled dead stick for a bobber, the rig was tossed out with a cane pole into a quiet eddy under the shade of a willow. When the bobber jiggled and finally went down, the supreme moment was at hand. No fancy routine, just lay back and haul whatever was at the other end out onto the bank.

This is not to say that artful techniques with worms don't produce probably better results. We just hadn't progressed that far yet. In later years, for small fish such as bluegills and other sunfish, rock bass, warmouths, and even for trout, I have never been of the school in favor of letting a lot of worm dangle. I believe in a thorough threading job, with the upper end pulled up to cover the eye of the hook, and just a short length of tail, double-looped and hooked so that it won't tear off easily, hanging off the hook point to wiggle. Worms do not live long after being hooked and dunked anyway. My theory is that changing baits often so that each is fresh and not sagging, and maybe a little big wiggly, is more important than how the worm is hooked. Further, too much dangle is an invitation, to small fish at least, to nip off the tail and leave it at that.

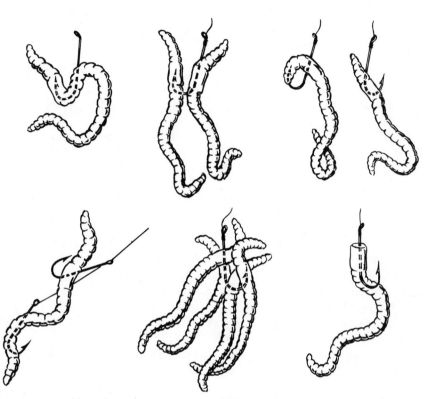

Here are some of the ways of placing worms on a hook.

Nonetheless, there are many varying opinions, and I seem to be in the minority where most written instructions about worm hooking are concerned. Some insist on hooking just a bit of the large end onto the hook, or on running the hook only through the so-called collar. Some let the hook point protrude. Some maintain that the barb and bend should always be buried. The accompanying drawings show several methods.

There is really nothing very complicated about the hooking operation. Once when I was a kid an old gentleman who fished the river near us was asked by another youngster: "How do you put a worm on a hook?" The old man looked at him and smiled and said: "Son, if you can't figure that out, you oughtn't to be fishin'."

The big night crawler is a different proposition from the ordinary angleworm. Except for very special situations no one would think of threading all of it on a hook. Crawlers are much tougher than worms. The common practice is to hook them through the prominent collar. The night crawler harness—described under "Equipment"—which has several hooks and stretches a crawler out, is a good rig. The method used by thousands of plastic-worm fishermen after bass nowadays, the one that has somehow

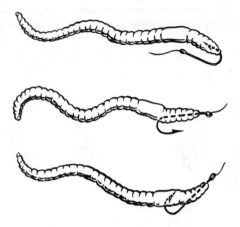

The so-called Texas rig for hooking plastic worms also works as well with a real night crawler.

picked up the name "Texas" rig, works very well with live crawlers. The hook is run straight down through the head and the crawler threaded on up the shank to the eye. The hook point and bend are then brought out of the side of the crawler, turned, and the point buried, to make it weedproof. Bury the hook eye in the crawler, thrust the end of a toothpick crosswise through crawler and hook eye, break off short, and the crawler will stay firmly in place.

When I fish worms for most panfish, I like short, fat worms of moderate size. I despise those ridiculously thin, hard-to-thread, break-apart worms all too many bait farms raise and peddle. I also like a light-wire, long-shanked hook. These are invariably extremely sharp and bend at a pull when hung up. Moreover the long shank allows ample threading room and is easier to extract. When panfish are biting eagerly, a worm of modest size allows them to grab the whole thing at once rather than just nibbling.

Nonetheless, there are exceptions. I have very seldom seen fishermen after big bluegills using large night crawlers. Yet an old friend of mine in northern Michigan, now deceased, years ago taught me about using these huge "snakes" in a deadly fashion for this purpose. We threaded on as much as we could get on the hook. The baited hook was trailed on a piece of monofil about a foot behind a good-sized double-bladed Indiana-type spinner to catch the attention of the fish.

We trolled with this rig, using oars and rowing very slowly along a weed bed, letting the bait deep. The fair-size blades, as they slowly turned, buoyed it up off bottom. The crawler trailed straight back from the hook. The second one of us felt a nip, we quit rowing and let out line, letting the bait and spinner drop back a couple of feet. Then, even without feeling more, we hit. Nine times out of ten, we had a big bluegill.

I want to repeat that in much of the north-country walleye range, even though this fish is a minnow-eater, for some unknown reason big night crawlers are often effective. A spinner with a treble hook on which a

Double or tandem blade Indiana spinner with night crawler trailing on footlong leader is great for big bluegills, bass.

crawler is looped is cast or trolled over walleye lairs. Just the crawler itself, cast and moved gently, often works well.

Crappies are not as eager to take worms as they are to seize minnows. Yellow perch will bite them, sometimes as readily as minnows. For white bass they are not very productive. Although small panfish-sized worms are also generally spurned by adult black bass, night crawlers—which the tremendously popular modern plastic worms imitate—are killers.

Both largemouth and smallmouth bass sometimes get on a spree of striking short at night crawlers, snipping off the trailing part and ignoring the rest. Long ago I devised a cure for this, especially when working on small-mouths inshore in spring on lakes, or in streams at any time. I used a thin wire hook with a small eye. About a night crawler's length up the line from the hook bend I tied in a small hook close to the line. I then threaded the crawler onto the end hook and forced it up over the eye and on up the line,

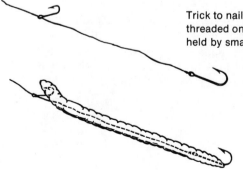

Trick to nail short-striking fish: crawler is threaded onto hook and up line, its head held by small hook tied into line.

81

where the head end was secured by the small hook. With a split shot or two, this rig casts nicely, looks good in the water and hangs every tail-nipping bass.

When you intend to manipulate a worm or crawler, not stillfish it, the priority rule is to use the smallest amount of lead necessary to get the bait down where you want it, or else to use a sinker type or a rig that allows the worm free play. I have long been an addict of the dipsey rig with a sinker at line's end, and a dropper about 6 inches long with a hook attached tied in to the line about a foot above. This setup casts easily, gets down where the fish are and allows the worm to wave freely. At the touch of a fish, a gentle relaxation of line removes any suggestion of pressure, and then the point is sent home. This rig can be crawled along bottom or used for bottom still-fishing. Undoubtedly there are others just as good, but this one is hard to beat.

The slip-sinker or fish-finder rig also is productive, but not in dense bottom cover. As already described, place a tiny split shot securely on the line a few inches above the hook and worm or crawler. This keeps the slip sinker from dropping down to the hook. Cast and let the rig lie on bottom. A fish picking up the worm will feel very little resistance as the line slides through the sinker. The strike can be made as the fisherman judges the instant is right.

Probably the most deadly worm and crawler fishing is contrived without any sinker at all, or else with only a split shot big enough to give a little casting assistance. Light spinning tackle handles this job best. On many occasions, using big crawlers, I've threaded one carefully and, with an open-face spin reel and light line, made a cast so gently the crawler can't possibly be flicked off.

After bass, I cast for example to a rock wall. I vividly recall a session of such casting on Table Rock Lake in Missouri. I was close enough so that a cast did not require much steam. The crawler would drop right against the wall. It was easy to picture it wafting down. When it stopped, usually resting on a ledge, I'd gently pull it off and let it tumble deeper to the next ledge. One evening I took a limit of bass, all in the 3 pound and up class, just this way.

On another occasion at Dale Hollow in Tennessee I became disgusted casting lures constantly and hardly attracting any smallmouth attention. I got a batch of crawlers and used this same technique, always fishing to a shady rock outcrop or the shady side of a steep point. It was pure murder. This is a mop-up method in trout lakes, too, using regular angleworms.

It is the swift trout streams that often present puzzles to worm fishermen. Here again, the idea should be to avoid weight and allow perfectly natural tumbling of the worm in current. The way to do that is to face and cast *upstream*. The method is not often used. I'll guarantee it will change your whole approach to stream worm fishing, whether for trout or smallmouths or even channel cats.

Depending on the size of the stream and its swiftness, you can either cast straight upstream or up and across. After the cast, keep the rod tip high, even holding it high above your head if need be. This helps avoid hang-ups on rocks. Keep reeling just fast enough to spool the slack as the worm drifts down. In a stream of modest gradient, don't use any weight if you can cast the worm. In a swift stream, use a split shot to help keep the bait deep. Fish take worms under such conditions with no nibbling—just a bang. Set the hook immediately.

There are probably numerous other unorthodox worm- and crawler-fishing techniques. Just because this bait is so common, and so appealing to fish, you shouldn't cease working out new approaches. But on those lazy days when you don't even want to think or exert yourself, simple stillfishing with a bobber, and a worm down below, one of the oldest approaches to angling, is still one of the most enjoyable and productive.

Frogs

Nowadays frogs are not as popular for bait as they once were. Part of this is due to the fact that most states have certain restrictions on the taking of frogs. There are seasons, and in some instances size limits. Frogs are not relished by all game fish, but they have always been a top taker of black bass. They also appeal mightily to pike, and very occasionally large frogs are used as muskie bait. What few anglers realize is that frogs are in addition high-priority forage for some trout.

Some of my earliest fishing memories concern fishing with frogs for bass. When I was a youngster artificial lures were not much used. Most anglers simply gathered bait of one kind or another and fished with it. A fishing uncle used to take my brother and me to small lakes near our home. The first order of business when we reached the lake was to go frog hunting. We had rigged up a couple of small makeshift nets from mosquito netting and willow switches. We carefully stalked frogs along the moist meadow of the lakeshore, popped the nets over them and then grabbed them with our hands.

The best bait frogs for bass, we soon discovered, were small ones that, when sitting, measured no more than 2 to 2½ inches from snout to rear end. We took great pains to keep the frogs alive in a wet burlap bag. A dead frog is not productive bait for most fish. However, frog harnesses are available in some sporting goods stores. Trussed in one, a dead frog is effective for pike and bass when cast and retrieved, although these harnesses are bothersome contraptions. We waited to bait up until we had found a spot that seemed especially likely to hold a bass. Nowadays of course almost all

Frogs can be hooked through lips, or through hind or front leg. The latter, not often used, allows frog more freedom of action.

fishermen would fish a frog with casting or spinning tackle. But those were cane-pole days, and I believe that fishing a frog with a cane pole is still the most lethal way to do it.

Some fishermen hook a frog through both lips. Others place the hook high in the meaty part of the thigh. Our fishing uncle had what proved over the years to be a far better idea. He used a slender-shanked hook and slipped it high up through a front leg. A frog thus hooked is able to swim well and act very lively. Granted, you lose a few frogs this way. The odd one gets free, or a bass jerks it off the hook. But in general the bass makes a vicious lunge at the swimming frog and engulfs it all at once.

Our cane-pole method was to drift very quietly into the edge of lily pads, or along a weed bed or near submerged logs or other hiding places for bass. The fisherman stood up front, reached out the pole and very deftly swung the frog out and dropped it with a plop. The moment it hit the water it started to swim. Very gentle pressure and manipulation caused it to turn in a circle, whereas a hind-leg hooking makes it appear tethered or held back. I recall one of those early sessions when we plopped frogs into small openings among lily pads and boated several dozen bass. There was no limit then. The cane pole was the perfect tool for hauling them out of the cover without entanglement.

This same basic method is still just as effective, whether or not you use a cane pole. Frogs should not be cast long distances, but simply tossed out into hot-looking spots. One time a few years ago I waded the shoreline of a Minnesota lake, moving slowly and silently among tall reeds. I used a 9-foot fly rod, baited with a small frog, and tossed it with an underhand swing out among the reeds, always close enough to shore so that the frog was instantly oriented. As soon as it dropped, it started for shore. Seldom did one get far before there was an explosion of water, and I had a bass on.

In a fast stream frogs are not very practical, but in slow, meandering rivers they can be murder, fished either from a drifting, carefully guided boat or canoe, or from the bank. I used to fish a smallmouth stream some years back that was gentle in gradient as most good smallmouth rivers are. It had so many deep holes that wading was impractical. I moved along the bank and tossed out small live frogs, using a limber spinning rod. It is easy to read the water from the bank and judge where a smallmouth should lie. As soon as the frog was in the water it tried to get to the bank. Any bass spying it knew the frog was in trouble. Since the frogs were small, even bass of modest size could gulp frog and hook on the strike. Certainly frogs are difficult bait to handle, but they do catch bass.

Larger frogs make productive bait for pike, but they should not be huge bullfrogs. Good-sized spotted meadow frogs seem to be the most lively, and at their maximum size—an overall stretch of maybe 7 inches—they can be easily handled even by pike of only 2 or 3 pounds. The technique is the same as with bass. Move the boat slowly and quietly and make short casts to likely pike lairs. You can't expect to handle frogs roughly and keep them lively. Use no sinker at all and keep the hook as light in relation to the size of the frog as is feasible for handling the fish.

Because brown trout have a broader range of diet than other trout, frogs can be used to fool old busters that often seem impossible to take otherwise. One good way to do this is to check big holes in a stream during summer evenings, just sitting and listening. During summer a big brown will take up residence in such a hole and live there for weeks. It seems to lose much caution at dusk, and commonly you can hear one sloshing around, feeding.

On one such hole I tried every trick I knew to conquer a brown that sounded like 5 or 6 pounds. I never did catch it, but perhaps foolishly I told a neighbor about the fish. We both lived near the stream. He went to the hole at dusk, eased a live frog with no weight on it into the upper end. Paying out slack, he let the frog drift down and attempt to make the bank. About halfway down, as it was related to me, there was a terrific commotion. The fisherman sat back and in due time he whipped the trout. As I had guessed, it was a good one, just shy of 6 pounds.

Frogs can be fished on bottom, too, but they cannot live very long there. A lively one dropped into a hole with weight enough to keep it down will struggle upward or to hide if possible and will take a good trout or bass. I once caught a big rainbow trout just this way while fishing for smallmouths that shared the stream with a few trout. Once the frog is dead it is not likely to be picked up, although if fresh-dead it may be. For catfish, fresh-dead frogs, allowed to lie on bottom, are excellent bait.

One time in the South I watched an old native set out a trotline for catfish, using frogs for bait in an ingenious manner. He used a short trotline and positioned it so that it was right at the surface. Each dropper line with a hook was about a foot long, and each was baited with a live frog hooked through both lips from beneath. The frogs incessantly moved at surface, creating small circles of commotion. He had the line loaded up with channel cats in no time.

Method of fishing frog just off bottom. Fairly heavy sinker keeps frog from returning to surface, but it keeps trying, and thus attracts fish.

I've observed catfish fishermen and also bass fishermen fishing a live frog on a casting or spinning rod, downstream, the fisherman standing in the stream. If the rod is held high, the frog is kept at the surface, struggling against the current. The action alerts any fish within sight of it.

Now and then one hears of toads being used for bait. I have never seen a fish caught on one and am convinced that fish won't eat them. The same is true, I believe, of tadpoles. A friend of mine who for many years owned a small northern lake that contained walleyes, bass, crappies, bluegills, and muskies made a careful study season after season on what the various fish ate. He opened stomachs, and he also was an intent and meticulous observer. I have seen that lake simply swarming with tadpoles. I have also read here and there that tadpoles are good bait. This man told me he had never seen any fish eat one nor found any evidence of such eating in stomach analyses. He was convinced the jelly-like tadpole contained some substance, possibly for its own protection, distasteful to fish. Possibly I'm prejudiced. Try toads and tadpoles if you wish, but I'm certain there are better baits.

Crayfish

Crayfish, or "crawdads" as they're popularly called, are not always easy to obtain in bait stores, but many anglers live in areas where they can gather their own. For general use for a wide variety of game fish there is nothing better. My earlier statement that small minnows are the best yellow-perch bait deserves some qualification here. In certain stony lakes where both perch and crawdads abound, crayfish 1 to 2 inches long make up a very substantial part of the perches' diet.

I remember an amusing occasion during a long summer RV trip when we camped overnight beside a small lake in North Dakota. It was "just another lake," not famous for anything. A youngster came by soon after we were settled, late in the afternoon, and asked if we liked to eat yellow perch. I figured he was about to give us some and told him we sure did. But he had a clever gimmick. He produced a 2-quart tin can about half full of small crawdads. He told us all we had to do was pay him a dollar for the bait, rent a boat from his dad and catch all we wanted.

It was such a good pitch that I couldn't resist. We had North Dakota licenses. The lad pointed out an area of the lake where he said we'd catch perch. He told us to just stillfish in around 10 feet of water. Just tear off the tail of the crawdad, don't bother to peel it, and thread it onto the hook. That we did. We used no bobber, just let the line down over the side to the proper depth. I can still see those perch. They bit like crazy, they were big and, because of the water hue, dark greenish and yellow. We sacked them up as fast as we could stay baited and had several wonderful meals.

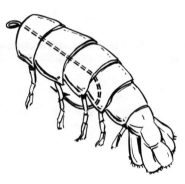

Unpeeled tails of small crayfish make prime bait for numerous species.

Of course the crayfish has attained its greatest fame as a bait for bass. But before we get into that, let me tell you about a trout-fishing experience. On a western trout tour one summer I ran into a gentleman on a famous stream who was lugging an astonishing catch of big trout. He carried a spinning rod, and I assumed of course that he had caught the trout on some small spinner or spoon. He quickly set me straight.

He had hanging from his belt a bait box filled with wet moss and some of the biggest crawdads I had ever seen. He acquired them, he told me, from a small, shallow, weedy pond, by pulling out weeds with a garden rake and picking out the entangled creatures. He also showed me what to do. The idea was to cut off the tail, peel it, then use the meat of a whole tail for bait.

Large peeled crayfish tails are deadly on big trout.

He had to quit because he was limited out, so he offered me the half dozen crawdads he had left.

I fished the first bait by casting up and across, using a single split shot and letting the bait tumble deep. When it hit the lip of a deep hole below and swung around, there was a jolting strike. I hit back, and a rainbow I bet would go 4 pounds took to the air. I managed to lose that one. But with the remaining five big tails I caught four big trout. I needed no further convincing. I suspect that some of the appeal is in the smell of the peeled meat, much as when peeled shrimp is used in saltwater. At any rate, I have used crawdads large and small on several occasions for trout, and each time with startling results. Some trout fishermen believe small whole crawdads are the best answer for high, cold, early-season water.

Panfish such as the various sunfishes and crappies do not eat crayfish to any extent, possibly because they do not readily come in contact with crayfish of a suitable size. However, I have gathered very tiny specimens, used the tails only and discovered that most of the sunfishes will avidly seize them as a stillfished bait. Redears, or shellcrackers, and yellowbreast sunfish take them more eagerly than do bluegills. Peeled tails, however, are good bait for any of the sunfishes.

In fact, peeled tails, stillfished, drifted, cast, fished on bottom, or even trolled, will catch most freshwater fish. Some fishermen are very successful with walleyes, using good-sized tails or whole crawdads. Whole ones, or unpeeled tails, are excellent bait for freshwater drum, a fish incidentally that is always highly underrated both as a fighter and on the table. Recently I caught several of moderate size in the slack glides of a swift stream where rocks make homes for abundant crayfish. In the same stream I also caught channel cats as readily on unpeeled tails as I did on worms. In some lakes and streams crayfish are abundant, in others there may be few or none. Wherever many are present, you may be certain they'll be utilized by many game fish.

As noted above, however, it is the appeal of this bait to bass that has long held it high on the list. Both largemouth and smallmouth greedily go after crawdads. The bait is strongly associated with the smallmouth simply because that bass lives in so many lakes and streams that are stony or rocky and thus an optimum habitat for both fish and forage.

I have often conquered hard-to-fool smallmouths in clear water by the simple expedient of casting out a whole crawdad with a slip sinker held a foot up the line by a split shot crimped on below. There are several theories about how to hook the bait and how to handle it. Some fishermen believe the hook should be threaded from the end of the tail forward and brought out up past the barb on the other side. This to some extent inhibits the little critter's movements.

Always hook from below through the tail. This does not noticeably injure the bait, nor much inhibit its movements. It also keeps the hook from hanging up among bottom debris or rocks. Some fishermen hook crayfish by slipping the hook under a couple of segments of shell on the tail.

Best way to hook live crayfish is through tail from beneath.

Many bait anglers break off the claws before using the crayfish. The little animals try to crawl under rocks to hide, and claw removal does slow them up. However, they usually try to move backward and in a free state always swim backward to escape. So probably the value of this practice is a moot point. I have never been convinced that the claws bother bass. Whole, heavily clawed specimens are commonly found in the stomachs of bass. Some anglers believe crawdads should be kept up off bottom so that they can't crawl under rocks. There are some instances where this is logical, but the crayfish is a bottom-dwelling creature and is therefore more natural there. Just move it every few minutes and it will stay in sight.

To get back to my simple smallmouth method. Cast the slip-sinker rig out and let it lie on bottom. A shoal with small stones is a good bottom, since smallmouth feed over these. Then you wait. Usually the bass doesn't smack

Some anglers break off the large claws before baiting with crayfish.

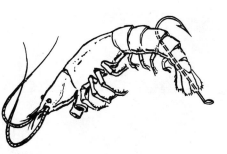

this bait and race off. It nips at it, turning it and fiddling with it. Then, with the bait in its mouth, it moves away. So, when you feel the first tentative nibbling, hold your fire. When the bass swims off, however, let the line slip through the sinker for just a moment, slack, then snug up and strike. Most of the time, you'll be hooked up.

A quiet fisherman who uses stealth, or an old-timer cane-poler, can mop up on bass by ingenious pinpoint drops of crawdads. The method works best in murky water, for you have to get close to your quarry, and in clear water you are liable to spook it. I learned the method years ago from a group of natives who fished on Buckeye Lake in Ohio. I couldn't believe the strings of bass they brought in and wangled an invitation to see how it was done.

One man didn't fish. He handled a paddle without a sound, easing the old wooden rowboat up to a spot where a stump protruded above water. Up front, the fisherman, standing, would reach out and drop a live craw-dad down next to the stump. By this method the fisherman has complete control, because his bait is on a short line. A bass would instantly seize the bait as it scrambled for cover. The fisherman then eased off a bit until the bass moved. Then he'd ram the hook home.

The same idea can be translated into making short casts while sitting in a boat, tossing the bait, without any sinker if possible, near underwater rock ledges, logs, or weed beds, then reeling it very slowly, pausing to let the bait work. Again, although now and then a bass will really slam it, usually it will mouth it first and then swim away with it, at which time the hook should be set.

As crayfish grow, they shed their shells. For a short time these "shedders" are soft to the touch, and when available, they make excellent bait. Probably because of the soft feel, all game fish seize them more quickly than they do the hard-shells. There are many different species of crayfish throughout the United States, and one or more are found almost everywhere. Be sure to check state laws about gathering them. In a few states they are gathered for commercial sale as a delicacy, and some of these states have seasons, and even limits.

Grasshoppers and Crickets

Both grasshoppers and crickets used to be strictly summertime baits. This is the season when they are abundant. But in recent years bait farmers have been raising millions of crickets, and they are for sale in some areas around the year. Both insects are so productive that they can be spoken of almost as one. They do not, however, appeal irresistibly to all game fish.

Bass, for example, will take grasshoppers under certain circumstances, even hoppers of modest size. Smallmouths are especially quick to grab them. But adult largemouth bass generally spurn any small offerings, unless they are short of food. As an example, I have watched bass in my own lake on our ranch turn down angleworms passed right under their noses. Yet big night crawlers drawn within sight elicited strikes.

I once caught a batch of hoppers, some small and a few of those very large ones no panfish could swallow. I pitched them out over bass plainly seen in clear water to observe the reaction. The small hoppers drew attention but no strikes. The big ones were occasionally taken when they moved.

The real forte of both grasshoppers and crickets is in filling stringers and creels with sunfishes and trout. One of the most famous and popular artificial flies for summer use, as most trout fishermen know, is the hopper. For bait fishing, using the McCoy is both great sport and exceedingly productive.

When my boys were small and learning to fish, I schooled them summers in northern Michigan by having them catch grasshoppers and fish very small streams. My theory is that if you learn to catch trout from a tiny rivulet, larger streams will seem easy. We'd creep up on a backwoods creek where brook trout were abundant. Few adult fishermen bothered with such streams. The trout were not large, but they were authentic native brookies, and wild. With hiding places at a premium, they were also wary. The boys, not very tall at that time, could do a fine job of sneaking up, walking gingerly so as not to shake the ground.

With either fly or spinning rod, and a half-rod length of leader or line out, they would ease the baited hook slowly and gently out above the streamside grass. Some of these creeks were no more than 2 feet across, yet most had fairly deep holes and of course undercut banks. The hopper was dapped onto the surface. If alive, it was allowed a short float. If dead, it was lifted and dapped again, as if it were trying to hop off the water. The way the brookies smacked them was phenomenal. There was no playing room. It was a matter of striking and lifting out the trout. Whether for youngsters or adults, the method is extremely productive.

All trout species will seize grasshoppers with alacrity. An excellent way to fish them in larger streams is to use light spinning tackle and a single split shot to assist the cast. If you are an accomplished fly fisherman, you can cast a grasshopper-baited hook. But you have to be gentle, else you'll snap the bait off. With spin tackle, the best way is to wade upstream, making short casts to treat the bait gently. The casts are made either straight up to the head of the pool, letting the hopper gyrate down through it, or on riffles or in shallow places up and across, so it will sweep naturally down. It is true that artificial hopper flies catch lots of trout. But the real thing catches more.

There are several ways to hook grasshoppers. To keep fair-sized ones alive and kicking, most fishermen use a fine-wire hook and slip the point in

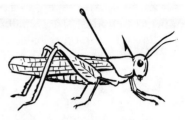

To keep grasshoppers or crickets alive and kicking, many fishermen use fine wire hook and run it from rear beneath collar back of head.

from the rear of the collar atop the back behind the head. The insertion should be shallow so as not to kill the insect. Even though there are a few kicks left in the hind legs after such treatment, I have never been sure it makes that much difference. When grasshoppers fall onto a stream surface, they float along, sometimes kicking, sometimes not. In either case trout take them. On a flat lake surface, gently casting one out with a fly rod, no split shot, and letting it make its small surface abrasions is, admittedly, most effective.

For much grasshopper fishing, however, I have often hooked the insect from below and up through the thorax. This gives a fairly solid hold. Most of the time I simply thread the hopper onto the hook, from the rear, bringing the hook point and part of the bend out through the tough thorax. This allows the hopper, though dead, to lie straight on the hook and appear natural. It can also be cast, with fly or spin tackle, without coming off, if you are reasonably gentle. This hooking method is particularly applicable for fly-fishing tackle, because you need no added casting weight. The hopper will float if you use a light hook, and a gentle twitch makes the bait lifelike. I think too much has been made — and repeated endlessly from book to book — about how to hook both hoppers and crickets. All fish that eat them will take them dead or alive. Fished below surface neither remains

I often hook hoppers from below up through thorax (top), or I simply thread them on from front or rear, preferably bringing the hook out below the thorax.

alive more than a few minutes anyway, and most of the time any method of hooking quickly kills them. Thus, simply put them on a hook in the way that best secures them.

Hoppers can be cast in late afternoon in shady places for bluegills, either on surface with a fly rod, or else with a spin rod and shot to let them sink. Stillfished, they are also one of the prime baits. Other sunfishes also grab them, especially the common sunfish. Smallmouth bass in both lakes and streams eagerly snap them up, above or below surface. There is no very special technique to be learned, except to be quiet and stealthy when fishing for smallmouths and to use fine leaders in the low, clear water of summer.

What has been said about hoppers applies in most respects to crickets. However, crickets are much softer and less sturdy, and it is difficult to cast them with fly-fishing tackle. Various books give all sorts of advice about how to put a cricket on a hook. Some anglers religiously hook them through the collar atop the back. It is virtually impossible to hook crickets gently enough so that they live for more than a kick or two, especially if you fish them underwater. Therefore, my belief is that it's a waste of time to go through the collar routine.

Last spring I fished for bluegills during the bedding season in May on Lake Toledo Bend on the Texas-Louisiana border. I fished with two local and very expert fishermen who are friends of mine. The male bluegills apparently had just arrived inshore and were fanning beds. Few females had yet arrived. Thus the males were in prime condition, fat and full of prespawning fight. But they were not in shallow water. Rather, we found them on a good bottom for bed making in 10 to 12 feet of water.

My two companions used the collar-hooking technique. But they often put two crickets on a hook as added enticement, which jumbled up the natural look quite a bit. I simply threaded mine on from the tail end, sometimes a single, sometimes two. We all used light spinning tackle and a single split shot, no float. Casts of course did not need to be long anyway. So far as I could see, there was no difference in the number of fish caught among us, but my hooking method lost fewer crickets to quick nips. Again I was persuaded, as we went in with a hundred or more big males that weighed very close to a pound each, that the cricket, alive or dead, is one of the best bluegill baits going.

Rock bass, warmouths, long-eared sunfish, green sunfish, common sunfish of course go for both crickets and hoppers as eagerly as bluegills. Sometimes yellow perch, and even white bass, will take them, but they like minnows better. As a basic rule, use hoppers of small to medium size for the sunfishes and the trouts, and for smallmouth especially in small streams; use outsize hoppers if you can find some for largemouth bass; concentrate on crickets for the panfish, and for low-water conditions on small streams for summer smallmouths.

Grubs and Caterpillars

There are all but endless varieties of grubs and caterpillars that make excellent bait. When digging for angleworms as a kid I used to believe that the occasional fat, white June-beetle larva unearthed was a good omen. It was certain to catch some kind of fish. Many confirmed bait fishermen get satisfaction from the challenge of picking up bait as they go, and baits in this category are common almost everywhere.

I have never cared too much for handling caterpillars, but many varieties of them do catch fish. In seasons when tent caterpillars erupt, a friend of mine pulls whole nests of them from branches and uses the worms for panfish bait. Because caterpillars are soft, they are difficult to hook firmly. Some fishermen try to hook them through the head, but this encourages fish to jerk the bait off without getting hooked.

Some of the most successful — and distasteful — bluegill fishing I ever experienced occurred one summer in Ohio. The fish were a bit difficult to catch in midsummer, long after spawning. But a local friend showed me how. Many years ago tree salesmen went through much of the Midwest peddling catalpa-tree seedlings. The fast-growing tree, they said, would make excellent fence posts. I don't recall many being used for that, but lots of catalpas were grown. A fat green butterfly larva found catalpa leaves a delicacy and came eventually to be called a "catalpa worm." These proved to be, and still are, one of the most productive bluegill baits imaginable.

However, my local friend insisted, if you cut into the worm and quite literally turned it wrong side out on the hook, so that the innards leaked off as it was dropped into a congregation of bluegills, it would catch three to one over just hooking the worm as it was. I confess this process never appealed to me. But it was true that chumming with the worm insides drew bluegills like a magnet. You could barely get a bait down before it was seized. Right or wrong side out, catalpa worms wherever found are known as a top panfish bait.

Wood grubs found beneath the bark of dead trees, or in rotting stumps, have long attracted bait-scrounging addicts. Golden-rod grubs found inside the galls, or bulges, on the stalks of that plant were first discovered as bait, I believe, by ice fishermen. Today they are used by summer fishermen, too.

Ice fishing in fact brought a number of grub baits to attention, several of them sold commercially. Mealworms and waxworms became very popular. Most places handle them only for ice fishermen. However, several years ago I discovered a source of preserved waxworms, used them for various panfish in summer and found them extremely productive. They are preserved in a solution and can be kept for long periods without spoiling. Perhaps other firms sell them, but the people who developed the preserving method and the only source I know are the Dickey Tackle Company, Land O' Lakes, Wisconsin 54540. They accept mail orders.

Mealworms and waxworms are larvae baits often used by ice fishermen. Preserved ones are now available and are excellent in summer for panfish.

Practically any grub or caterpillar—except the hairy ones—makes good bait, mostly for panfish and trout. Numerous very small grubs work fine, but few anglers bother with the tiny hooks and fine lines needed in order to use them properly. Here and there written information about bait fishing has shown how to lace soft caterpillars to a hook instead of threading them on. Incidentally, this same sort of information has been bandied about relating to grasshoppers and crickets. If you think about it, in the time you spend tying a hopper or a caterpillar or grub to the shank of a hook, you could just as well be catching half a dozen fish by using an angleworm! It seems to me simply too much bother to pursue such intricate ideas for presentation.

Nonetheless, it is interesting to scrounge around your own area seeking new baits in the grub and caterpillar categories. The search may lead you to sources you've never considered. And on occasions when you are out of bait, knowledge of some of these offtrail ones may come in handy.

Hellgrammites and Other Nymphs

Nymphs represent the aquatic larval stage in the metamorphosis of certain flying insects. They are found under rocks and stones in streams and lakes, and some of them in the mud of lake shallows. One of the largest, the aquatic stage of the horned corydalus or dobsonfly, is commonly called a hellgrammite. Although these are not always easy to find, they are sensational as bait for numerous fish.

Hellgrammites hooked under collar
stay alive a long time.

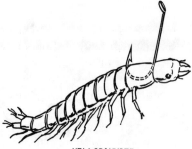

HELLGRAMMITE

Most hellgrammites are at least 2 inches long. Some are much larger, 3 inches or more. They live under rocks in streams and along lakeshores. Early in summer they crawl out of the water and make small cells under stones or debris nearby, eventually entering the next stage, the pupa, and finally emerging as a large flying insect. In the aquatic stage they are tough, leathery creatures that are renowned as bait for smallmouth bass. They also appeal mightily to trout, largemouths, walleyes, and perch.

As many a first-timer gathering and using hellgrammites has discovered, their jaws can inflict a painful nip. The tough collar behind the head is the place to grab one, and it is also the place for the hook. Run the point and the bend under this collar and the bait will stay on well and also remain alive for a long time.

I have used hellgrammites on several occasions for both trout and bass. One problem in fishing them is that if you drop the bait on bottom it will crawl under something and hide. Thus the best way is either to drift one on a free line in current, or else to use a bobber or casting bubble that will hold

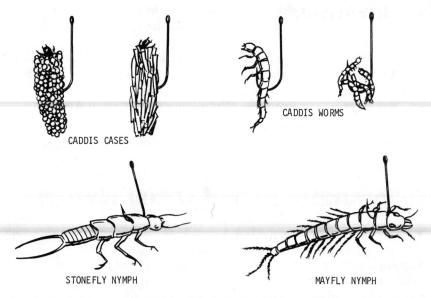

CADDIS WORMS

CADDIS CASES

STONEFLY NYMPH

MAYFLY NYMPH

Other nymphs make fine baits.

it near, but not on, bottom. On a trout stream a hellgrammite drifted through a deep run below a bobber is almost sure-fire.

There are many other varieties of nymphs, smaller but just as deadly because they are a staple of the diet of many fish, from trout to bass and sunfishes. Stonefly nymphs, the small wormlike nymphs that live inside caddis cases made of small debris, mayfly nymphs – which are sold to ice fishermen under the name "wigglers" – are all most effective items.

Some bait stores handle certain nymphs, or you can easily gather your own. In streams a common gathering method is for one person to thrust a screen into the current while another a short distance upstream kicks over stones and rocks. The loosened nymphs float down and catch on the screen, where they can be picked off. Abundant mayfly nymphs can sometimes be shoveled up in bottom mud near a lakeshore.

There is nothing complicated or special about fishing methods when using nymphs. For the smaller ones, very fine, small hooks must be used. Stillfishing with a bobber just as with angleworms, or else drifting free or under a bobber as described are standard approaches. The tiny caddis worms, when pulled from their cases, look very inconsequential. But if you thread one on a very small hook, use a fine leader, flip it upstream and let it drift back as you take in line, you'll discover that these (or any other small nymphs) are among the favorites for trout.

Salamanders

One spring on a fishing trip to Tennessee I saw a man coming in off a lake with an unbelievable string of smallmouth bass. I couldn't resist asking the standard question about what he caught them on. He told me, "spring lizards." It turned out that the little critter he called a spring lizard was a salamander or newt. He gathered them from under rotted logs in the woods and in other such moist, dark, woodsy places.

A year or so later, fishing a beaver pond in the Great Lakes area that I knew contained some big brook trout, I was having so much hang-up difficulty with lures that I began scrounging around for something to toss out under a bobber as bait. I remembered the salamanders. In a few minutes I was able to find three of the quick creatures, of a slender, reddish variety about 3 inches long including the tail.

I hooked one through a front leg, as the Tennessee bass fisherman had instructed, and tossed it out. Although this was a terrestrial species – some kinds are aquatic in the larval stage and have external gills – it was very lively in the water. For a few seconds. Then the bobber literally swooped under and away. I was hooked up to a beautiful brook trout of close to 2

Small terrestrial salamanders are sensational bait for trout, bass, and other game fish.

pounds. Each of the other two salamanders produced likewise. I had certainly learned an important bait lesson.

Salamanders and their relatives the newts are found in many varieties and have individual species ranges. One or another is present in most parts of the United States. Some are only 2 or 3 inches long when adult, but others may be 1 or 2 feet or more. Some species live out their lives on land, in varying moist habitats, but a good many breed in water, and the young go through a larval stage in water, usually with external gills. Most kinds have feet even in the larval, aquatic stages. A few have only two rather useless feet.

Not many anglers are aware of the excellent bait qualities of salamanders. Small, land-based varieties are particularly effective on trout in spring when water is high, but they are also productive on almost any game fish. Terrestrial adults can be found under wet leaves or beneath rotted logs near almost any lake or stream. Aquatic larval salamanders are common in shallow ponds and in swamp and slow-stream waters, but finding and collecting them is not exactly easy.

Salamanders are scaleless and come in numerous colors. One type is even black with bright yellow spots. Although anglers may have reservations about handling them, there is no need to be squeamish. They are harmless, and actually most interesting, creatures. Most are fairly tough on a hook in their larval stages. But some terrestrial adults are fairly fragile and also capable of shedding most of the tail at will. So these should never be hooked in the tail except high up at its base. One with a broken-off tail will, when free, in due time regenerate it.

For a number of years several lure makers have designed plugs that supposedly represent large aquatic salamanders. One of these, I believe, was dubbed a waterdog. It took some time, however, for bass fishermen to catch on to the fact that the real waterdog is a sensational bait for largemouths. Although aquatic salamanders of various species range over most of the United States, one large species, the tiger salamander, is

Adult tiger salamander (top) and larval stages with external gills (below). The aquatic young, called "waterdogs," have become extremely popular in a number of large western bass lakes.

especially abundant in several of the western states. This creature lives as an adult on land but breeds in shallow pools and ponds. The so-called waterdog is a larval stage of this salamander. It has external gills during that stage but loses them when it changes to land-based adulthood. (Several other species are called waterdogs in other areas of the United States but are seldom used as bait.)

I have seen shallow ponds in Colorado, way up in the mountains, literally swarming with waterdogs. A few years ago someone tried these as largemouth bait, and they were sensational. A large seining business grew in several western states, with thousands of waterdogs trucked to boat dealers at lakes such as Mead, Powell, and other western desert impoundments in which they appear to be especially deadly.

Most larval waterdogs available from bait sellers are 4 to 6 inches long. All four feet are developed, and the creatures will cling with tenacity to any surface or crawl beneath cover when fished. Experienced waterdog fishermen hook the salamanders upward from the bottom through both lips. They can then be cast just like a lure. Use only enough weight to get the dog where you want it, on bottom. Then the technique is to keep twitching the rod tip to move the bait a few inches at a time. This alerts bass and also keeps the salamander from hiding. When a hit occurs, give a little slack to allow the bass to take the bait, then hit hard.

Waterdogs, and other salamanders, are often picked up by fish as they are sinking. Therefore free-lining with no weight is sometimes an effective method. I have used this technique several times with small terrestrial salamanders, fishing for both trout and bass. You have to keep a close watch on the line and note the slightest twitch as the fish picks up the bait, but you shouldn't keep the line snug since this inhibits a pickup.

Although waterdog fishing has become a popular and productive bass-fishing method in the Southwest and West, it is not practiced to any extent elsewhere. There are several other large aquatic salamanders that could be utilized as effectively, if anyone would ferret out their breeding places and

99

A few southeastern bass anglers have discovered the fantastic bass-catching properties of an aquatic salamander called the siren.

try them. And the so-called "mud puppy," which grows to a foot long and is a larva throughout life, is found over most of the eastern half of the United States.

A few southeastern fishermen have realized the fantastic bass-catching properties of an aquatic member of the salamanders called the siren. Actually there are several species among the sirens and the so-called mud sirens. They are found in the vegetation and mud of Florida and Gulf Coast ponds, rivers, and swampy lakes, and for some distance up the eastern coastal states in similar habitats. During the past few decades as the water hyacinth all but took over numerous Florida and other waters, at least one of the sirens has taken up abode in the roots of this plant.

They're difficult to collect. Some people gather them by wading with a box frame with a screened bottom. The box is shoved under the edge of the hyacinth bed and lifted. Individual plants are thus raised up, and the sirens, attempting to escape, drop into the box and are retained by the screen. This two-footed, slender, snakelike salamander grows from 6 inches to a foot long. It is the striped variety. Some others are much larger.

Sirens are tough creatures and very lively on a hook. They can be hooked through the lips—be careful not to place the hook into the head, which will kill the creature—and slowly trolled some distance behind a bottom-bumping dipsey; or they can be stillfished beneath a bobber. Most anglers knowledgeable about siren fishing—and they are few—use no sinker for this method. The salamander will try to get into the bottom mud anyway. It should be held of course off bottom. Tail hooking is usual for stillfishing along hyacinth and lily-pad edges among tall reeds or cane. Deleting the bobber and casting a tail-hooked siren into grass flats and other lie-ups of bass, then letting it swim free, is also effective. The bait must be moved every few seconds to prevent it burrowing into cover.

Some astonishing catches of large bass have been accomplished by the use of sirens and western waterdogs. I would suggest that more attention be paid to these creatures as bait for both bass and trout, and possibly for other species as well. They tend to be abundant, at least locally. There is a large area of bait fishing here that has not been as thoroughly explored as it should be.

100

Salmon Eggs and Roe

Almost all fish are to some extent spawn-eaters, and therefore the use of fish eggs for bait has long been a well-known, popular, and effective method of bait fishing. Most notorious of spawn-eaters are the salmons and trouts. This is partly because salmon and trout eggs are of good size and extruded into places where they are rather easily found and gobbled up. Thus most roe and egg fishing is done for trout, especially for the steelheads of the West, but also for the so-called steelheads of the Great Lakes region, the big rainbows which move out of the Great Lakes and into streams in spring. Other trout of course will eagerly take salmon eggs or roe sacks — browns, cutthroats, brook and lake trout. Some states have from time to time outlawed salmon-egg fishing on certain waters, so it is advisable to check the regulations before using this bait.

I vividly remember the run of husky rainbows that occurred each year when I lived in northern Michigan near the Sturgeon River. In due time of course salmon eggs became a favorite fishing method. I remember an amusing incident of a man standing on a side-road bridge across the river, tossing single salmon eggs into the stream below, where several trout of 5 or 6 pounds were easily visible. They snapped up the eggs, and then finally he pitched out a single egg with a tiny hook in it, attached to monofil line. It, too, was snapped up. The gentleman landed several trout just that way, perhaps not very sporting, but admittedly effective.

Salmon eggs were eventually outlawed in Michigan, but in the interim the spawn bag had found its way from the West Coast to Michigan steelhead streams. Whenever anyone caught a female trout full of roe, it was saved, and clusters of eggs were bound into a thumbnail-sized fine-mesh bag, at that time usually made from a piece of nylon stocking. This was tied to a hook, or in some cases a hook was tied or thrust into it. Bags of fresh roe are sometimes more productive than preserved salmon eggs, because juice and scent from them leach into the water.

If you intend to use single eggs, or clusters in a net, be sure to check state laws where you fish, to make certain this is legal. Most of my own fishing in the beginning was of the single-egg type, using preserved salmon eggs. This is common on the Pacific Coast and of course can be done anywhere inland for trout other than steelheads. It is something of an art. Small, short-shanked, gold-finish hooks with a turned-down eye are made especially for single-egg fishing.

To briefly review single-egg rigging for stream fishing: use a small slip sinker on the line, and a very small swivel at line's end over which the sinker can't slip. To the other end of the swivel, tie a light leader, as light as you think can be used without losing big trout. This leader should be about 18 inches long. The small hook should be almost completely buried in an egg. Preserved salmon eggs are best for this because they are fairly tough.

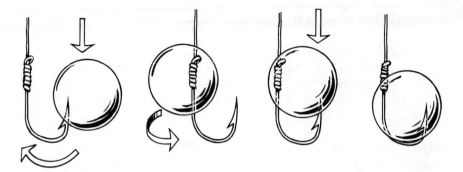

Steps in properly placing salmon egg on a short-shanked hook.

Thrust the hook point through one side and out the bottom, then turn the hook enough to bring the shank and eye clear down inside the egg. Next swivel the bend around and push the hook point back up into the egg. Properly done, this places the barb and point inside the egg, and the lower curve of the egg rides within the bend of the hook. The rig is cast and allowed to bounce along bottom. A trout that picks up the egg will strip line through the slip sinker without much drag. The fisherman should strike immediately.

Modern clusters are often placed in special net material available in stores in steelhead territory. Usually the fine net is dyed red, and the thread that ties the top is also red. Most anglers fish clusters—commonly called "strawberries"—the same way as single eggs. I have often tossed a cluster upstream and let it tumble back through a pool, keeping slack up just enough to feel a strike. Or, it can be cast across a big, deep hole and allowed to swirl around. Fishing it on a tight line downstream is never very effective.

In addition to being used in these rather specialized methods, salmon eggs make excellent bait simply stillfished in trout lakes. They can be tossed

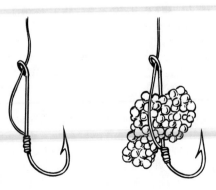

Method of snelling hook to hold gob of salmon eggs.

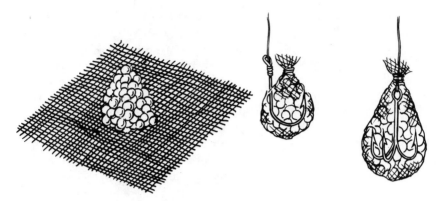

Egg clusters can be tied in small squares of porous fabric.

out and allowed to sink, or used below a bobber. Obviously the slip sinker is not needed for lake fishing.

Other Baits

All of the baits covered so far are more or less standards. They are by no means all that are available. As I mentioned earlier, the search for new ones that produce dramatically is an intriguing hobby and challenge. It is also most interesting to ferret out obscure baits that have become traditional in a given area yet are all but unknown elsewhere.

One winter in Florida I was trying to catch some of the outsized yellowbreast sunfish that I knew swarmed in the Suwannee River. I wasn't doing much. It might seem that sunfish should be easy to catch anywhere. Big old ones are not, and the yellowbreast is commonly very wary when old. A weathered wooden, flat-bottomed boat eased along the shore near me, and the occupant kept making short casts toward the bank, sort of lobbing out some bait that I couldn't identify.

What I did make out was how his rod bent every few minutes, and, when he strung a sunfish, how many he had. The size of some of them was phenomenal. When he got close, I praised his ability. He told me ability had little to do with it. The bait was what counted. He was using the meat of freshwater mussels. He gathered the mussels, kept a batch in a bucket in the boat and opened them as needed.

Part of the meat of any mussel is tender and tears away easily or is thrown off a hook. But a portion near the adductor muscle is tough. The bits that fly off on a cast simply chum fish to the hooked portion. Later I used mussels of one variety or another for various species all the way from Florida to the Great Lakes area to Texas.

I presume grasshoppers, which we discussed earlier, can be considered "flying" insects. But they are rather special. Many other flying insects are also sensational bait. I chuckle when recalling a session of fishing for big cutthroat trout on the Yellowstone River in Yellowstone Park when a heavy salmon-fly hatch was in progress. This large insect is actually a stonefly. Trout gorge on them during the large early-summer hatches in the West.

Everyone was frantically casting artificial flies. Some people were occasionally catching a trout. A fellow with cowboy boots and a Texas license on his car was sitting with his wife on the bank. They held, of all things, cane poles. I talked to him. He confessed he knew nothing about trout fishing—except (he allowed) the blamed things were ridiculously easy to catch. They had eight big cutthroats on a stringer. He was simply baiting a small hook with the real insect and beating every fly fisherman on the stream.

Cockroaches, which are classed as flying insects, make excellent panfish bait, although some anglers are prejudiced about handling them. Some beetles make fair bait. So do dragonflies. My most amusing experience with flying insects—and I think it showed a certain ingenuity—concerns a hatch of big mayflies on a slow stream loaded with brown trout.

The current was so slow that the browns could look over my artificial dry flies and turn them down, taking the real flies instead. I tied on a small, very light hook of fine wire. I cut a thin sliver of cork from an old cork bobber and forced it up onto the hook shank. Atop the cork I daubed a bit of chewing gum. Then, catching a large mayfly, I gently stuck it to the gum. Believe me this is a delicate operation. But the fact was, when I floated the invention down over the trout, with the mayfly moving its wings a bit, it was instantly engulfed. I wouldn't want to go to the bother very often, but I did catch a mess of good browns that time just that way.

A freshwater bait that is seldom used, and in fact seldom even recognized as one, is the leech. Strange as it may seem, leeches are classified among the true worms and are quite close relatives of the earthworms. They are mostly aquatic, dwelling in muddy pools or in wet, swampy places. Sometimes they are present in lakes and slow streams.

When I was a kid I knew them well, but not for fishing. My brother and I used to wade and swim in a creek on our farm. Invariably we found a leech or two attached to our hide when we got out of the water, and blood ran when we pulled them off. We always called them "bloodsuckers." Indeed, leeches are bloodsucking worms, attaching themselves to fish, turtles, snails, and to any land-dwelling creature that wades into their bailiwicks. The common variety, available over a broad area of the United States, is seldom over 2 inches long, but it can stretch to twice that, or snug up to a fat half-inch.

Very occasionally a bait shop may have leeches to sell. They are not easy to gather. Once a partner and I, hunting turtles to eat, gathered a glass jar full by pulling them off the legs and shell openings of the turtles. Leeches are astonishingly productive bait for numerous panfish, and moreover they are one of the toughest baits in existence. Impaled, a leech will stretch and contract and wriggle, and you can catch fish after fish on the same bait. Stillfishing or casting one with very light tackle and slowly retrieving are good methods to use. This is a bait, incidentally, seldom if ever used for trout. Tumbled along a riffle or through a pool, it is a lethal offering. The same is true for stream smallmouths.

Freshwater Baits

Some freshwater fish have a highly varied diet, while others feed predominantly upon only one or two items. Largemouth bass, for example, will eat at times almost anything that moves. Conversely, in most walleye lakes minnows make up 90 percent of the diet. Availability often dictates what fish feed upon. This may sometimes mean seasonal abundance of a certain type of forage. The walleye in some lakes feeds avidly during certain seasons upon mayfly nymphs on bottom and even takes adult hatching insects on the surface. The chart listings here of freshwater fish and the best baits for each are not intended to imply that other baits won't sometimes produce. Baits listed are simply those considered most effective most of the time.

Largemouth Black Bass	night crawlers, minnows, frogs, crayfish, large grasshoppers and nymphs of aquatic insects, salamanders—in fact almost any bait available.
Smallmouth Bass	night crawlers, minnows, crayfish, frogs, leeches, adult insects and aquatic nymphs.
Bluegill	worms, crickets, various insects and aquatic nymphs—small minnows appear occasionally in diet, but not to any extent.
Common Sunfish	same as bluegill, but inclined more to bottom feeding.
Yellowbreast Sunfish	same as above, but also readily takes small minnows.
Shellcracker (Redear Sunfish)	worms, crayfish tails, small mollusks.
Crappie (both White and Black)	minnows.
Rock Bass	worms, small crayfish, minnows.
Warmouth Bass	same as rock bass.
Sacramento Perch	worms, crayfish, minnows, insects.
Rio Grande Perch	worms, minnows.
White Bass	minnows.
Yellow Bass	minnows.
White Perch (of eastern U.S.)	worms, nymphs, small minnows.
Walleye	minnows, night crawlers, crayfish.
Sauger	same as walleye.
Yellow Perch	minnows, worms, mayfly larvae, crayfish tails, leeches.
Muskellunge	large minnows.
Pike	minnows, frogs.
Chain Pickerel	same as pike.
Atlantic Salmon	seldom if ever fished with bait, and in many waters bait fishing is illegal for it.
Landlocked Salmon	smelt.
Chinook Salmon	pilchard and other small baitfish, fresh or frozen, cut herring.

Freshwater Baits (continued)

Silver (Coho) Salmon	candlefish, herring, cut herring.
Rainbow Trout	worms, night crawlers, minnows, spawn, insects.
Steelhead Trout	salmon eggs, in some places night crawlers.
Kamloops Trout	baitfish such as kokanee.
Cutthroat Trout	same as rainbow trout.
Brown Trout	same.
Brook Trout	worms, night crawlers, minnows, nymphs, leeches, small salamanders, crayfish tails.
Dolly Varden Trout	minnows, spawn, cut bait.
Lake Trout	smelt, minnows, cut bait.
Grayling	small insects, aquatic nymphs, salmon eggs.
Rocky Mountain Whitefish	aquatic nymphs.
Lake Whitefish (all species)	bits of worm, small grubs, cut bait.
Cisco	small minnows, cut bait, mayfly nymphs.
Smelt (eastern variety)	small minnows.
Mooneye, Goldeye	small minnows, insects.
Channel Catfish	worms, minnows — wide variety of baits.
Blue and Yellow Catfishes	whole baitfish, or cut bait.
Bullheads	worms, cut bait.
Carp	occasionally small worms, nymphs.
Buffalo	worms.
Suckers (all species)	worms.
Squawfish	minnows, cut bait, insects.
Freshwater Drum	worms, crayfish, various mollusks, cut bait.
Bowfin	minnows, crayfish.
Burbot	minnows, cut bait.
Gar (all species)	baitfish alive or dead, cut bait.

Saltwater Baits and How to Fish Them

THE WORLD OF SALTWATER bait fishing seems at first appraisal radically different from that of fresh. Tens of thousands of lakes and streams inland are individually compact ecological communities, in any of which the total number of predator and forage species is rather limited. Even the largest impoundments renowned chiefly nowadays for their largemouth black-bass fishing are mere droplets of water compared to the vast sweeps of the oceans and their inshore bays and beaches.

Indeed, the world of saltwater really is an extremely complex one. It is interesting to note that a large percentage of the acreage – some biologists estimate as high as 75 percent – of numerous freshwater lakes is used hardly at all by its resident game fish. It contains little or no supply of food. Conversely, some of the most desirable species of saltwater, such as the popular kingfish or king mackerel, the bonitos, tunas, dolphins, and many more, are what is known as pelagic species – fish of open waters. Food of some kind is available almost everywhere in saltwater.

Some of the open-water species, lacking a swim bladder by which idle suspension in water is possible, must swim constantly from the time they are hatched to the day they die. These are endlessly avid foragers. They must be, to stoke their high metabolism rate caused by ever-working muscles. They are also chiefly migratory, moving into warm southern waters in winter and pushing north with the spring as the water warms in that direction. This also is a necessary way of life, because at low water temperature their reduced metabolism rate could not sustain their endless motion.

The number of game species in saltwater is larger by far than in fresh. The variety within any particular saltwater habitat is also usually far larger. Predator game-fish sizes also have greater variance, and the oceans are home to fish much larger at maximum than those in freshwater. A largemouth bass of 10 pounds is a bragging fish. Many sea basses (another family) grow to several hundred pounds. Yet there are also scads of inshore

107

marine panfish such as the grunts, various small snappers, and others that are not much larger, and some no larger, than the so-called panfish of freshwater.

The infinite variety in saltwater is one of its high appeals. The experienced saltwater angler knows this. He may be fishing for one kind of fish and in the process catch a dozen other species. The freshwater fisherman visiting saltwater for the first time, or only occasionally, is often inhibited by this. How do you go about fishing such seemingly endless expanses that all look alike?

Well, to begin with, they are not by any means all alike, although marine habitats fall into certain rather limited basic categories. There are the offshore waters—the blue-water fishing territory, the open waters of the Pacific, Atlantic, and Gulf of Mexico. Here dwell the big sharks, the marlins and sailfish, the tunas and various members of the swift, streamlined mackerel family, big jacks, dolphin, and down on the deep offshore reefs such species as red snappers and amberjacks. Next comes a broad coastal strip that might be termed near-shore waters. Many of the offshore species occasionally visit here, where they consort and overlap with others such as tarpon, bluefish, cobia, barracuda, and various groupers, which stake out these waters as one of their favorite swimming grounds.

Many of these inshore species also move commonly into the channels and b s, over the grass flats or among mangrove islands, although they might not be considered as varieties specifically of protected waters. Nor are they true species of the surf, the beach-bordering swath along any open shore. Game fish that feed in the surf along and off sandy beaches are exemplified by striped bass, channel bass (redfish in some areas), whiting, pompano, sometimes croakers and drums, and on the Pacific the corbina and some of the surf perch. But not all shores are open expanses of sandy beach. The rocky areas on both coasts have their own highly specialized denizens, not strictly surf species but those that dwell more or less permanently among the rocks. These are exemplified by the rockfish of all but endless variety of the Pacific Coast.

Then there are the inside waters, the protected bays and channels, behind barrier islands and reefs. This wonderful fishing world is the richest of all and is where by far the majority of saltwater anglers operate. Some of the highly varied and numerous bay species move offshore during certain seasons, or even spend some periods in the surf, and to some extent in inshore and occasionally deep offshore waters. But the average angler knows them in the bays and channels—the weakfish and its ubiquitous spotted southern relative affectionately known as the speckled trout, the channel bass, in some places the striped bass, the black drum, sheepshead, snook, some of the jacks, in places numerous tarpon, bonefish, croakers, snappers, and a galaxy of small pan-sized denizens. Some of the sharks also are common in bays.

These then are the basic divisions of saltwater habitats. The enormous extent of them, taking in the length of two coasts and the mass of the Gulf of Mexico, each latitude with its own permanent and migratory residents but with much overlapping also, would seem to make marine bait fishing a conundrum. It really isn't that perplexing.

For one thing, the majority of anglers on any of our three major coastal areas — Atlantic, Gulf, Pacific — seldom fish consistently more than a modest stretch, and in that region individuals usually specialize in one habitat or another, and in only a few favorite fish species. An angler in New England may be an addict of cod and pollock, one from New Jersey or that general region may have a fixation on bluefish, or weakfish, or tautog. Some care only about striped bass. I've known scores of Florida and Texas anglers who habitually fish only for speckled trout and redfish. Of course most of these fishermen catch other species as incidentals. But the point is that for any individual angler saltwater, though seemingly vast and complex, boils down to a domain no more complicated to approach than fresh.

One interesting reason is that even though the forage creatures of saltwater are infinitely varied in form and species, the bulk of the diet of marine fishes is really rather spare in basic variety. Large numbers of marine species utilize to a large extent the same fairly simple menu. The thousands of species of insects and their nymphs and larvae consumed eagerly and in huge bulk by freshwater fish are virtually nonexistent in marine environments. Marine fish are to a large extent more voracious in their feeding than freshwater species and are seldom if ever quite as selective. Theirs is a vast, fish-eat-fish world. The diets of marine game fish are certainly far more oriented toward forage fish and each other's young than is the case in freshwater.

Thus, live fish or pieces of fish will catch almost any marine gamester in any of the several habitats. Certainly some of the species do show preferences — a sheepshead will grab a fiddler crab quicker than it will a live baitfish — but all told marine fish are seldom as choosy as their inland cousins.

In addition to fish, marine predator species come in contact within their several specific habitats mainly with forage from two other huge groups of animal life: the mollusks and the crustaceans. From these three groups comes most of the food of marine game fish.

Mollusks of course are those creatures whose shells — sometimes empty, sometimes with the living animal inside — are cast in legion upon the beaches or lie in the bottom mud of bays. Oyster, clam, conch, scallop — as shell collectors know, there are thousands of varieties. Some fish are equipped to crush shells. Among them are the drums, the croakers, the tautog so well loved by anglers along the Atlantic from Cape Cod to the Carolinas, the sheepshead. But many of the species that are not specifically mollusk grubbers will eagerly pursue a chum streak laid down with ground clams and just as eagerly seize a hunk of mollusk meat an angler has thoughtfully shucked for it, and in which he has schemingly buried a hook.

Although you may not realize it, the squid, a prime marine bait in numerous places and for many varieties of fish, is one of the mollusks. Its "shell" is inside, a stiff piece of material that gives form and stability to the body.

The crustaceans number among their many species one of the most productive of all saltwater baits, the shrimp. It is at least close to true that you can catch any saltwater fish on a shrimp, or a piece of one. Also in this huge animal grouping are the crabs. Fiddler crabs, small green crabs, the hermit crab with its soft, elongated body that uses a cast-off mollusk shell for its home — these and many other locally abundant crabs are eaten by, and used as bait for, most of the game fish of inside waters, of the surf, and occasionally even in inshore and offshore waters. The sand flea — there are a number of varieties — is also a member of the crustacean group, and a common saltwater bait. When I lived for some years in California, most of them spent on or near the beaches, this was one of my favorite "scrounge" baits. If you were quick about it, you could always grab a sand flea or two as an incoming wave subsided, and they'd intrigue almost any fish that fed or moved in the surf.

In addition to baitfish, mollusks, and crustaceans, there are the marine worms that take the place in saltwater fishing that is filled by the angleworm and night crawler in fresh. These worms — bloodworms, clamworms, muckworms, etc. — are found in numerous species along all our coasts. They are the marine aquatic varieties of the true worms — actually relatives of the earthworm. They are not popular everywhere but are used widely along the northern half of the Atlantic Coast of the United States, and to some extent along the Pacific. Eels, present along the Atlantic, are also a prime bait, again chiefly over the northern half of the East Coast.

Thus, even though the varieties of baitfish may be many and the species belonging to the mollusk and crustacean groups legion, nonetheless the fundamental list of saltwater baits is really not as long as that of the baits utilized inland. Further, the prime baits most popular and productive at any given place along any coast are usually fewer than those that inland anglers are used to fishing.

In Part 2, "Rigs for Bait Fishing," I explained that generally speaking those used in saltwater are replicas or rejiggered combinations of those for fresh. However, components for salt are ordinarily heavier and may differ in design. Most saltwater fish are much stronger and tougher than their inland relatives. On the other hand, for the smaller marine species of inside waters, rigs are just about identical to those of inland waters. There are vastly more freshwater than marine anglers, but no one with only inland experience needs to be inhibited by the awesome expanses of saltwater. In many ways bait fishing in salt is really simpler than its freshwater counterpart, and the fish are often less wary.

An influential phenomenon with which marine anglers must deal is the almost constant motion of the water. Inlanders new to salt seldom realize how complex and continuous are these movements. Tides of course are the prime movers of the medium. Fish are sensitively attuned to tidal motion. I remember how impressed I was years back when I had my first winter of fishing the numerous tidal cuts and canals of the Everglades in Florida. Action might be near zero. No fish could be seen moving. Then suddenly there came a stirring beneath the mangroves. Long before a tide reached miles inland to drop or raise the water level noticeably, the fish felt the tidal pull and became more active.

Every bay, brackish river mouth, canal, and salt marsh is touched daily and for hours at a time by tidal movements. The same is true of course of the surf and the entire open oceans and Gulf. But this is only one of the movements. Over the vast sweeps of saltwater the air is seldom utterly still. Winds add to water movements in shallow bays and on the blue water outside. The surf sets up its own complex currents, waves pouring in and moving back, sucking water from the beach in intricate undertow patterns and hurling it back seconds later upon the sands.

Further, numerous currents, some well charted and some whimsical, run throughout inshore and offshore waters. Sometimes two of these butt into each other, leaving long drift streaks—heavy debris of gathered plankton and other drift items—on the surface and meandering for miles. Commonly charter-boat skippers seek these drifts. I have often seen drifts where on one side the water was a translucent green, and on the other a vivid crystal blue. Game fish feed avidly in the drifts and some kinds just off them on the blue side.

I mention water movement because inlanders new to saltwater all too commonly envision large expanses of placid water, particularly in bays. This is a misconception. There are calm places at certain times, but the oceans are seldom still. Thus bait is moved and animated here more than in freshwater lakes. Astute anglers learn to use the currents, to carry a bait where they want it, to drift chum to fish that will follow it to a bait, to help present a bait in a motivating manner.

They must also be keenly aware that to anchor a bait where you want it to stay, or to keep it from moving where you don't want it to go, may require heavier sinkers, or angular sinkers (the pyramid). Furthermore, the wear and tear of saltwater movement can be abrasive to lines and leaders, rubbing them against rocks or shell or barnacled pilings. Thus, a knowledge of currents in any given favorite spot—a pier, a jetty, a stretch of surf, a reef miles out, a grass flat in a bay—becomes important. These will sometimes dictate the kind of bait you use, and often how you present it.

At the end of Part 4, just as at the end of the discussion of freshwater baits in Part 3, you will find a list of all the saltwater sport fish and the favored baits for each. This is only to give you a quick and easy reference, so that if you go after a species new to you, you will know what it eats as mainstays and what most anglers use to catch it. This by no means infers that many of the listed species won't accept other baits. When in a pinch try whatever is available in bait shops or can be scrounged along shore. Maybe something not on the list may work wonders.

Saltwater Baitfish

Almost any small marine fish can be considered useful as bait. But, just as in freshwater, there are certain ones that have attained high popularity over the years. Some of these are rather regional. Obviously certain small fishes useful as bait range over only a portion of the several thousand miles of coastline of the Atlantic, the Gulf, and the Pacific, or else they are heavily utilized over only a small portion of their range. Others have more extensive ranges, including both coasts.

The list of useful marine baitfishes is long. It would be impossible in fact to attempt to deal with all of them. Further, some of them belong to families containing several dozen species, of which any or all may be used at one location or another.

Most bait species that have attained high popularity belong to groups that are natural forage for numerous saltwater fish. A number of these are small fish that feed on plankton and tiny marine organisms. They form an important step in the food chain of the oceans. They convert plankton to rich fish flesh upon which the predator fish depend to a large extent for a livelihood. Most of them are schooling varieties. They commonly appear in enormous concentrations, close-packed near surface, and layer upon layer below, with literally millions of individuals in the vast group.

In such situations these helpless creatures are an open invitation to decimation by voracious predators. So the forage varieties become a staple item of game-fish diet and are therefore favored for bait by anglers. Another consideration invariably is availability to the fisherman. Some marine anglers catch their own baitfish, with throw nets, dip nets, traps, or even hook and line. But the commercial bait business is so well organized and such an economic force in many coastal communities today that baitfish are usually abundantly available in shops.

There are several important properties to appraise in baitfish for saltwater. Silvery coloring is one. Any small, silvery fish, alive or dead, is easy for game fish to see and may attract a hungry customer because of its flash. It is interesting to note that most of the massively schooling plankton feeders are brightly silvered. It is almost as if their coloring is designed to attract predators, so that they may fulfill their planned destiny to serve as a vital step in the marine food chain.

Numerous saltwater fish have oily flesh. This is particularly true of the small, schooling plankton-eaters, and of many predaceous fish that feed upon them. This is another important physical attribute that should be looked for in baitfish. Firmness of flesh is also advantageous, so that the bait will stay on a hook, not be easily washed off by waves or surf, or torn off by short-striking game fish. However, most of the oily baitfish are rather soft. So compromises must be made. Any bait with tough skin obviously offers solid hooking advantages, even though its flesh may be somewhat soft. Marine anglers sometimes lash baitfish to a hook if they are too soft to stay well in place otherwise. This practice of course is followed usually only for large, "important" game species. It would hardly be worthwhile for fast-hitting smaller kinds.

Although many saltwater fishermen employ live baitfish, more probably use fresh-dead and frozen bait, which would appear to enjoy far greater popularity in saltwater than in fresh. I recall fishing one year for chinook or king salmon out of Monterey, California, for several days and on several different boats. Each used fresh-frozen whole sardines of good size for bait. On another occasion a few years ago I fished out of Everett, Washington. Again, frozen, neatly packaged baitfish were used.

It must be remembered that handling live baitfish and keeping them alive in quantity for saltwater use is not quite as simple as taking a bucket of minnows along, or seining them on the spot, for freshwater bass fishing. A boat must be equipped with an aerated bait tank of substantial size and much care used, on long hauls especially, to keep the baitfish alive. Further, a major share of fishing in saltwater with whole baitfish is done by drifting or trolling, allowing a bait to waft down in offshore water with a light sinker or none, or letting it drift on a moving tide. The character of the big water and the current movements make possible the use of fresh-dead or frozen baitfish in a manner that makes them appear either alive or else crippled and therefore easy forage for a game fish. A tremendous business in frozen bait has thus been built up over the years, and for numerous game species this works as well as living baitfish. It's certainly far less bother.

The use of pieces of fish, which among saltwater fishermen are usually spoken of as "chunk bait," and of fillets, in most cases with the skin on, called "strip bait," is much more prevalent among marine anglers than inland. These will be covered in a later section. I mention them here because some varieties of baitfish are seldom used alive. Their major role is for cut or strip baits, and sometimes as ground chum. Some varieties are used in all ways.

Most of the "minnows" that serve as bait in freshwater come from only two or three fish families. The situation in saltwater is quite different, partly because of the expanse of that environment and the broad range in size and variety of predator fish. Further, the forage species themselves are far more highly varied. In addition, whereas chubs, shiners, and suckers are used throughout most of our inland waters for bait, on the marine coasts a forage fish present in one place may be absent in another.

It may be helpful, therefore, for reference purposes, to deal individually, if briefly, with some of the more prominent baitfish species used alive, fresh-dead, frozen, or as chunk or strip bait. This should give inlanders new to saltwater an introduction to what to look for in baitfish, and inform experienced coastal anglers about some of the baitfish most effective outside their bailiwicks.

Menhaden. This is a member of the large herring family. It moves in vast schools, ranges the Atlantic from Brazil to Florida and north to Nova Scotia. It has long been an exceedingly important commercial fish, most of the catch being utilized in stock and poultry feeds. It is an extremely oily fish, and some of the catch is used for making oil. But the menhaden is also one of the top baitfish of the Atlantic Coast, especially from Chesapeake Bay northward. It is a prime natural food of all the predators—bluefish, sharks, striped bass, the tunas, and many others of offshore and inshore waters. Small specimens are fine for live bait, but since its flesh is very soft, this forage fish is utilized mainly for cut and strip baits and also, ground up or otherwise, as chum. Some of the commercial catch goes to the bait business along the coast.

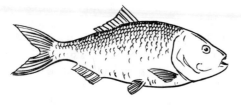

The menhaden is one of the top baits along the Upper Atlantic coast. It is oily, is used alive, as strip bait, or ground for chum.

Mullet. There are numerous mullet species. On our coasts these fish range from the New England region south and throughout the Gulf down to Mexico. In the Pacific the chief range is from about the mid-California coast southward. The heaviest abundance of mullet is found along the lower Atlantic Coast to and around Florida and all along the Gulf Coast throughout the Texas portion.

Mullet gather in schools large and small. Like the menhaden they feed fundamentally upon plankton, mosses, and the lower food-chain items. The mullets are heavily fished commercially, especially along Florida, where they are considered a standard food fish. Curiously, on the western Gulf and along Texas in particular no one would think of eating a mullet.

The flesh of the mullet is firm but oily, and its skin is tough. These attributes make it a perfect bait. Mullet are natural prey for a broad spectrum of game fish. They grow to a fair size, 12 to 15 inches or a bit more. Some of the large ones are used whole for large marine gamesters. Sometimes they are gutted and sewn to hook and leader. Smaller live mullets are highly productive, fished in the bays and channels or from piers, and also in the surf.

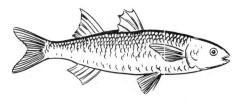

Mullet, with firm, oily flesh and tough skin, are popular for bait on both coasts. They are used alive, dead, whole, strip-cut or chunked.

I remember throw-netting 5-inch mullet in a tiny tidal pond on the beach of Padre Island, Texas, where they had been trapped by a falling tide. We hooked them through the caudal portion of the body, just ahead of the tail fin, and turned them loose in the surf. This proved murderous for large redfish.

Mullet are also used as a fresh-dead and as a frozen bait. Probably mullet baits are most commonly found in the form of chunks or strips. However utilized, this is one of the most important saltwater baitfish.

Killifish. Several species of this family are used for bait. The common killifish is renowned as a live bait, especially along portions of the upper half of the Atlantic Coast. Eastern anglers often call these small fish of shallow bays and marshes "mummichog." The full range extends from the Gulf of St. Lawrence to the Gulf of Mexico. The average bait killifish is about 3 or 4 inches long. They grow to roughly 6 inches maximum. Killifishes are renowned as important controls on salt-marsh mosquitoes. They feed avidly upon the larvae.

Called by easterners "mummichog," the killifish is an important, tough live bait along the upper half of the Atlantic coast.

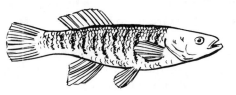

This bait is often used alive because it is exceptionally tenacious, withstanding rough usage and drastic water temperature and salinity changes. In fact, some anglers carry these tough little baits simply buried in wet seaweed or wrapped in wet burlap. This is a baitfish commonly caught in minnow traps in shallow lagoons, baited with a chum of bits of crab or clam. Even on a hook the killifish stays alive longer than most other small marine baitfish.

Anchovy. Usually fishing books refer to this baitfish as the "northern anchovy." This family of small fishes is fairly closely related to the herrings, but all anchovies are in a family of their own. Although there are anchovy representatives along both Atlantic and Pacific coasts, it is on the Pacific that these baitfishes are truly important. They are used chiefly for albacore,

115

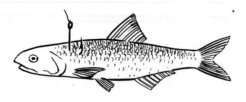

The anchovy is a prime bait particularly along the pacific, where it is used both alive and frozen for numerous game fish. It is often hooked under the bone that forms the shoulder.

yellowtail, barracuda, and a few other prime game fish of the Pacific Coast. In fact, several thousand tons of anchovies wind up in the commercial bait market annually along the California coast. Some are used alive on large party boats for a number of game fish, others are available frozen.

There is also a small baitfish of the Atlantic Coast called the striped anchovy. Striped bass, various tunas, bluefish, and the mackerels utilize it as a natural food, and it has substantial standing as an East Coast baitfish.

Anchovies are on the average 4 inches or slightly more in length. They are dark-fleshed, oily baitfish, and the bones are rather soft. They tear easily, die quickly on the hook and must therefore be changed often. Nonetheless they are extremely effective. They are heavily used whole and alive or "pinched" to cripple them, and are even used as cut bait.

For all of the smaller baitfishes, attention must be given to where best to place the hook. The delicate anchovy is often hooked under the bone that forms the "shoulder," above the pectoral fin and behind the cover of the gill. Certainly other hook placements are used, but this spot holds the fragile bait best.

Sardine. The sardine so well known as a tinned commercial product is actually a member of the herring family. On the Atlantic Coast the canned sardine is the young of a species of herring. However, the Pacific sardine properly bears the sardine name even though it is of the herring family. It is much used on the Pacific Coast, where it is often called a pilchard. It is an open-ocean fish that moves in vast schools. It is oily and rather soft. Sardines are therefore generally hooked through the snout, which is quite tough. A high percentage of bait sardines are marketed frozen. However, live young sardines are an offering commonly used by large-boat anglers after mackerel, tuna, and such open-water species. It is also used as cut bait.

Along the Pacific the sardine is often called pilchard. Both live and frozen sardines are popular. Sardines are hooked by most anglers through the snout.

The small silversides is a common bait along the upper half of the Atlantic coast.

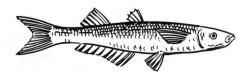

Silverside. Some species of this fish are found in freshwater and others in saltwater along the upper half of the Atlantic Coast in near-shore waters and estuaries. It is small, adults averaging about 3 inches. They are fairly easily seined or dip-netted in shallow water on low tide. Silversides are used whole, both alive and dead, and occasionally as cut bait, for numerous predator fish of the region.

Flying fish. There are several different species of flying fish used for bait. One or another is found in the Atlantic, the Gulf, and the Pacific. These are open-water fishes. Their chief use is as a deep-trolling bait for large pelagic game fish such as the marlins. They are fished whole, hooked through the lips or with hooks placed inside the body and projecting. Sometimes they are surface trolled also, skipped along. This is a tough and durable baitfish. Most anglers use it only on charter boats or if they own a large ocean-going big-game fishing craft.

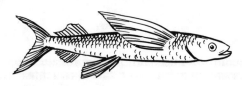

Flying fish make tough bait, used whole for trolling, usually for open-water big-game fish.

Needlefish. These slender, elongated, long-beaked fish provide excellent bait when small. There are species on both coasts and in the Gulf. In the Pacific they are present along the southern third of California. They are abundant in the Gulf and about Florida. It is in the warmer waters that they are most prevalent, although some do reach as far north as Cape Cod in the Atlantic.

Needlefish are found in the warmer waters along both coasts, and in the Gulf. Often they are used dead, for trolling. Small, live needlefish, hooked through the rear body and allowed to swim free, are deadly.

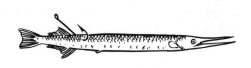

Small needlefish are fished alive, although trolling with dead ones is also productive. Some years ago in Florida I recall learning what excellent bait they were by netting small ones that would home in around a skiff while I was fishing near Sarasota. We'd hook them through the back or across the meatier rear part of the body, then let them swim free. This is too much of a temptation to almost any predator species.

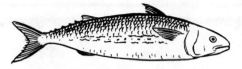

The common mackerel is bait for a great many fish on both coasts.

Mackerel. Mackerels of several varieties are used whole as baitfish for the large open-water game fish that habitually prey on their schools such as tuna, sharks, swordfish, marlin. Bluefish, striped bass, cod, and almost any of the more voracious predators eagerly slam into schools of the smaller mackerels and cut them to pieces. Thus the mackerel of one or another species is a standard bait on both coasts. They are used whole when trolling for large game fish. However, cut and strip baits from mackerel are what most anglers utilize and ordinarily come from frozen stock in bait shops, although occasionally local anglers catch their own and cut it fresh.

The Pacific mackerel is trolled whole and used for strip or cut bait.

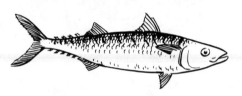

Ribbonfish. This baitfish deserves attention here because it is such a standard nowadays along the western Gulf Coast, especially Texas. "Ribbonfish" is a misnomer but is so firmly established that the name will probably never change. The fish is actually a cutlass fish. (The true ribbonfish belongs to another family.) The cutlass fish is extremely long and slender, the body severely compressed. The narrow jaws are set with astonishing fangs. The bright platinum-silver hue of this fish and its strong, oily flesh, plus its abundance along Texas in large schools, have made it one of the most used of all baitfish there. It is a standard on charter and party boats, where whole, dead (frozen) specimens about a foot long are strung on a multiple-hook rig. Packaged frozen in cut chunks it is also a prime bait item for pier and bay fishing nowadays.

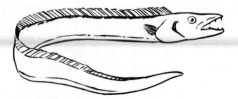

The name ribbonfish is a misnomer; it is actually the cutlass fish, important as a baitfish along the western Gulf.

118

I have caught ribbonfish that were as much as 40 inches long with artificials and with cut bait. They are amazing fighters and leapers in their own right. During chilly winter weather they congregate in protected spots such as inside-water boat basins and ramps and are netted by tons for bait.

The foot-long dead specimens, hooked and dropped overboard and allowed to sink with little or no weight, and to drift wherever current is running, undulate temptingly almost as if alive. In clear offshore waters they can be seen by roving predators for some distance. Recently on a party boat 40 miles out in the Gulf out of Port Aransas, Texas, I saw kingfish (king mackerel), dolphins, sharks, big jacks, blackfin tuna, and several other species caught on this bait in a couple of hours. Ribbonfish are also ground up and thrown out as chum.

Other species. The bait species described so far are representative of those much used, but there are endless others. Some of these of which a marine angler should be aware I'll mention briefly, so that readers perhaps so far unfamiliar with them will be informed when they hear the names.

The slender balao is a member of the halfbeaks. Its under jaw is much extended. It is a most important baitfish on both coasts, usually trolled for any of the large open-water game fish.

The slender balao, a member of the halfbeak family, is usually trolled whole for large game fish.

On the Atlantic and Gulf, the common silver perch, whole and alive, is a popular bait.

Silver perch of the Atlantic and Gulf are a common bait used often whole and alive, hooked through the tail. The queenfish of the Pacific is a popular live bait. The bones that attach the pectoral fins are sturdy, and commonly the hook is run under one, forward of the base of one fin. Butterfish and a small species of the Pacific Coast colloquially called a "tommy croaker"—incorrect for "tom cod"—are popular on the West Coast. Butterfish are

Along the Pacific the queenfish serves as a baitfish. It is best hooked under the bone that attaches the pectoral fin.

Butterfish are used whole on both coasts, but especially on the Pacific for yellowtail.

The tom cod, common inshore along the Pacific, is a prime baitfish.

sometimes a hot bait for the immensely popular Pacific yellowtail. Another species is a popular Atlantic bait, whole, for big bluefish and other inshore varieties.

The pinfish, a bright-hued panfish reminiscent in shape of the freshwater sunfishes, is an abundant denizen of protected waters mainly around Florida and the entire Gulf Coast. It is a popular bait among tarpon fishermen, used whole and alive, hooked under the dorsal as a rule. The goggle-eyed scad, and other scads, serve as tarpon bait in eastern waters, and for several predators of the Pacific.

The bright-hued pinfish, alive and whole, is particularly attractive to tarpon.

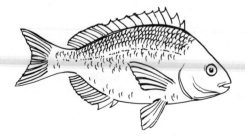

Several saltwater smelts are prime bait, especially on the Pacific Coast. Whitebait smelt and the eulachon or candlefish, an exceedingly oily smelt, are among the best known ones. Whole small sheepsheads, blue runners, grunts, snappers, various nongame croakers, even sea catfish with the spines clipped, serve as bait for specialized purposes or because they are readily available. Almost any small fish or piece of it produces.

I recall with great pleasure and some amusement how some years ago I often fished lazily in Florida, perhaps from a bridge or in some well-protected water, for lowly grunts. I have never needed big fish to keep me happy. And I discovered, being the sort who likes to try eating practically anything that will take a hook, that the various grunts are superb panfish. On light tackle they are also good little sport fish.

The goggle-eyed scad, and other scads, serve as tarpon bait in the east and for various Pacific predators.

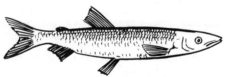

The whitebait smelt is a Pacific bait of some importance. It is an oily species and eagerly taken by game fish.

I'd begin by scrounging around for almost any bait I could find. Then I'd patiently wait out catching the first grunt. That first one didn't go on the stringer. It was cut into bits to catch more. Then when I cleaned the catch for cooking, I'd hold out one. This reminded me of how countrywomen, until early in this century, would get a batch of "starter" or yeast from some neighbor or on their wedding day, for baking bread. It was partially used as needed, regrown in a warm place and carried wherever one moved. My grunt-for-grunts bait served as a continuous starter, one fish saved from each batch caught, so that I could endlessly keep going.

Not all the rigs for saltwater covered in detail in Part 2 are suitable for use with baitfish. To quickly review the ones that are, consider first the bobber-and-sinker rig. Tarpon anglers often use a big bobber to suspend a live baitfish below. A myriad varieties of saltwater fish in the panfish size are caught by this simple setup, the only difference being in the smaller size of all the components.

Drifting a live baitfish along a jetty or pier, or on a tide, or simply drifting it with breeze or current in a bay, is a most effective manner of using live bait suspended beneath a bobber. The popping-cork rig that I described in detail, though used as a rule with shrimp, is also effective with small baitfish. It is most often used in the shallow water of bays. However, where currents run in channels, or even along piers, the motion given to a baitfish alive or dead by jerking the popping cork intrigues some game fish.

The underwater float with a sinker above it can be advantageously used at times with baitfish. It forces the bait up off bottom away from nibblers, keeps it from trying to hide and places it where game fish can easily see it. The three-way-swivel rig—a standard surf rig—commonly employs a live baitfish. And the fish-finder setup is perfect for one because it allows the bait to swim at will.

One of the best setups for small to medium fish is the simple one where the sinker is placed at the end of the line and a live baitfish is fished on a dropper some distance above it. This can be cast or fished vertically over the boat side. The problem in casting live bait is that you have to be gentle or you kill the bait or cast it off the hook. Certainly where you can just let a bait go, that is, swim free with only a small weight or none at all—in the Pacific sometimes called "flying"—chances of success are high. I've already mentioned letting mullet baits swim in the surf. You can fish other baitfish the same way in bays and from piers. Some of the Pacific charter boats habitually use live anchovies with little or no weight, sometimes dropping them over after chumming up a school of albacore or yellowtail by pitching other live anchovies over the rail. If you cast a live baitfish, try to "lob" it out to avoid snapping it off the hook.

A good rule to follow is to cast a live baitfish as little as possible. If you can get it to the fish without hard use, so much the better. Dead baitfish, fresh-dead or frozen, are often cast and retrieved. They can be rigged with multiple hooks or trussed to a hook, or the line can be run lengthwise through the body with a needle so that they stay on. It makes little difference during retrieve, if an angler gives them enticing motion, whether they are alive or dead. As has been noted, many baitfish are trolled by marine anglers. These trolling baits are almost entirely fresh-dead or frozen.

It will be advantageous to any saltwater fisherman to study the baitfish he most uses meticulously in order to determine how best to hook it. Trial and error will show which hook placement—lips, snout, shoulder, under the dorsal, in the tail—holds any given variety most securely, with least damage. In addition, sometimes finicky game fish turn down bait with one placement but will eagerly grab it when the hook is differently placed. Be alert to this phenomenon and experiment.

Much depends on how hardy the baitfish variety is, and how and where it will be fished. Obviously there are only so many placements for a hook. Hooking a mullet through the caudal peduncle, that is, the muscular part of the body to which the actual tail fin is attached, works well. But a suspended baitfish, such as one fished below a bobber, may stay in a better

This sketch shows the several places in which a baitfish may be hooked. Where the hook is placed depends on how the bait is fished.

position if hooked at the front of the dorsal fin, in the middle of the back or barely aft of the dorsal. Take care not to injure vital organs. Lip hooking— through both lips—is a common method. Most anglers bring the hook up from below the chin. A number of live-bait anglers in saltwater also hook small baitfish crosswise through both eye sockets.

You have to consider currents in relation to how you hook live bait. If you fish an inlet with a stiff current running, dorsal or tail hooking won't let the bait look natural, and it will die rather quickly. Fish invariably lie or move with head to current. Thus lip hooking a live bait presents it best in current and allows it to stay alive longer.

If you are new to saltwater, don't think you must have a foot-long baitfish even to catch a big predator. To be sure, the slender ribbonfish I described earlier in this section are often used in 1-foot size. But this is because of the build of the fish. A mullet that big would all but choke many a game fish. For most saltwater game fish—there are a few exceptions—a live baitfish 6 inches long is considered a big one. Such good-sized baits can be fished in outside waters, or inshore, by very slow trolling or by drifting, the latter being a most productive method. Large dead baitfish are rigged in various ways by charter skippers and other blue-water fishermen to make them appear natural as they are skipped on surface or trolled. Sometimes the backbone is removed, and they are trussed to the buried hooks.

In a few marine-fishing situations really large baits are used, I've seen a 6-pound sheepshead placed on a great steel hook with a chain and swivel attached, to catch a 400-pound jewfish. Large sharks are often caught on baitfish of several pounds. But these are such specialized endeavors that the average angler will seldom be involved in them, and if he is he will undoubtedly have expert advice or else learn as he gains experience.

Chumming

Chumming refers to the use of bait put into the water to attract game fish to the area where the fishing is to be done. The angler I wrote about in Part 3 who stood on the bridge and tossed salmon eggs into the stream to incite big rainbow trout lying below to gobble them up, then slipped them one with a hook in it and a line attached, was chumming. Chum is any bait material used to draw fish and, hopefully, hold them so that the hook can be presented.

In some instances live baitfish are used as chum. This is common on the big party boats along the California coast. In other cases fresh-dead baitfish may be employed, or chunks of fish. Other baits such as shrimp, alive, dead, or in pieces, are also used for chumming. More common, perhaps, over all the marine-fishing territory is the practice of heaving overboard chopped or ground bait. Ground leftovers of baitfish, often from those that have been frozen and then thawed a little too long, so that they are too soft for the hook, are pitched by the quart over the rail of party boats.

Ground or shredded clams are a common chum along the Atlantic Coast. The refuse left from cleaning fish is also often ground and used as chum. Chopped or ground menhaden and mackerel make excellent chum because they are oily. Ground chum invariably leaves an oily slick on the surface, and the particles drift down, oozing juices and scent into the water. Any predator fish is certain to investigate.

Chumming is not much practiced in freshwater, but it is not only common in saltwater but a very productive specialized use of bait. In open offshore water large game fish can be brought up from deep water by chumming. This is the way large tuna are often brought up into an area where they will see the bait. Not long ago, fishing on a large, plush party boat, the *Scat Cat,* out of Port Aransas, Texas, I watched the skipper anchor 30 miles offshore, then heave much ground chum overside. Following that he dropped a number of ribbonfish over. In a few minutes the area was well stocked with several varieties of predaceous game fish — sharks, kings, dolphin. Thus the chum, spreading out by wave and current action, located the game fish and brought them into fishing range.

Chumming is also an excellent method of locating, and gathering, bottom-feeding varieties, such as flounders. It is likewise effective in collecting such species as sheepsheads. For example, a coastal fishing partner and I have often used a boat hook to scrape and chip barnacles and other marine growth from pilings. The shower of chumming debris settles, and then hooks baited with shrimp or fiddler crabs are let down. The sheepsheads have been drawn as if by a magnet and are waiting and ready. Chum not only draws fish to a given area, but it invariably arouses them so that they become eager to feed.

One of the most important uses of chumming, besides attracting fish, is to hold them so that baits can be presented. For example, some of the schooling game fish of the Pacific are spotted by a lookout on a boat and their position and general course relayed to the skipper. The boat makes a quick run to intercept, ahead of the moving school. Chum is dribbled overside — live or fresh-dead baitfish as a rule. The maneuver is used to grab the attention of the school. The boat moves slowly ahead a short distance, leaving what old hands call a "short chum line." The intent is to entice the school into following and staying near the boat, so that the fishermen can get into them.

In attempting to raise fish from deep water or to locate them when none are sighted or known to be near, a boat may lay down a "long chum line" of several hundred yards. In this type of chumming, lines are usually put over and hooked baits let well back. Thus the baits are trolled right in the chum line. If there's a hit, or wallowing fish are sighted, it's a sure sign fish have been tolled in. The boat slows and stops, and some further chumming may ensue while fishing begins. Often live baitfish are purposely injured before their use as chum near the boat. The crippled forage is hesitant to leave the vicinity of the craft, and this urges game fish even closer in.

Experienced users of chum do not put it out haphazardly. In fact, there is something of an art in how it is handled. For example, weakfish enthusiasts on the East Coast anchor during an incoming or ebbing tide in a spot where a strong tidal current runs. The fish are already active on the moving tides. The fishermen drift chum such as live shrimp down the current and of course have baited hooks over, hanging in the swath of tidal flow. The weakfish are mesmerized by the chum and come straight to the bait.

Currents are always charted and employed even out in blue water to make certain the chum goes where it will do the most good, and that the fishermen will be able to take advantage of its position and appeal. In chumming for bottom fish in water of modest depth or in shallows, of course it is desirable to find quiet places if possible. Then chum can be deposited on bottom over a given area and won't drift away.

A most interesting variant of chumming is practiced on occasion at night with the aid of lights. The lights are used to attract shrimp and small fish and hold them as natural chum in the lighted circle. The forage in turn draws the predator species, and the angler has them right where he wants them. A classic example of this occurs at Port Mansfield, Texas. A fee-operated fishing pier uses lights, which attract shrimp, which in turn attract speckled weakfish (trout). Some prodigious catches are made.

Several years ago I went with two partners to Port Mansfield, and we crossed Laguna Madre in a boat and entered the land cut that at this point slices across Padre Island. We set up camp on the south bank of the cut. This cut is a deep-dredged canal or channel that reaches from the bay to the Gulf, so that tides are allowed to run through each way. This allows fish passage and also helps to prevent the shallow bay waters from becoming unduly saline from evaporation.

We had with us a small generator and gasoline motor secured to a plank. The generator was to be wired to a pair of sealed-beam head lamps. These we had fixed to a crosspiece nailed to a tall, sturdy stake. We thrust the stake into the sand, tilted so that the lights would be focused on the water as darkness closed in. Presently the tide was racing through, transforming the cut into a swirling river.

The little motor put-putted away, the generator poured out current to keep the lights bright. In no time swarms of shrimp and small baitfish were circling and gyrating in the glow. Groups of trout moving through the tide paused to feast on this bonanza—and found some shrimp with hooks inside. During one run of tide the three of us caught, cleaned, and iced down in boxes we'd brought for the purpose some two hundred specks. It was great fun and marvelous eating for weeks after. But we were so tired we fell on our air mattresses laid on the open sand and didn't stir until the sun blasted us awake as it climbed the sky late the next morning.

Cut Bait

Chunk baits. Chunk baits are pieces of fish cut any way the fisherman desires. The general idea is to use a piece of fish in such a way that it stays solidly on the hook. Chunk-cut baits are used widely in saltwater. Almost any marine denizen will accept a piece of fish. Some of the top game species fall for fish chunks in a pinch, and with many of the less discriminating varieties this kind of bait is all anyone ever needs.

Scores of times I have fished from a pier, run out of bait such as frozen shrimp, then put pieces of one of my catch to work as bait. In fact, many marine anglers fishing for a variety of species often keep any nondescript small fish they happen to hook incidentally—a small jack crevalle, a pinfish, a nongame hardhead croaker, even the lowly sea cat—as an ace in the hole when bait runs low. Of course standard baitfishes such as mullet, mackerel, sardines, and many others are also used as standard chunk-cut bait.

Most bait of this type is fished for bottom-feeding species. It may be still-fished or reeled slowly along bottom. It is also fished almost everywhere at times in the surf. A chunk of mullet used with a standard surf rig or a fish-finder rig in the surf will often take as many channel bass as will small live mullet. For fish of small or modest size—the hordes of species that can be lumped together as saltwater panfish—bits of fish seem to be just as productive as expensive live baitfish or shrimp.

There is nothing complicated about fishing chunk-cut baits. Practically any of the saltwater rigs described earlier can be utilized to present a chunk of fish. As I've said, almost any fish can be used for this purpose. I've fished on red-snapper boats and watched deck hands take a very small snapper off a hook, a fish too small for the ice, carry it back to the bait preparation table and cut it up to use as a good tough bait to catch more snappers.

A baitfish of modest size and slender outline may be steaked and the chunks hooked across through skin on both sides.

There was no point in letting it go. After being brought up so quickly from a depth of a couple of hundred feet or more it would die in a few minutes anyway.

Although any fish will do, certainly the oily ones make the best chunk bait. Half a sardine or anchovy is a standard chunk for many West Coast anglers. However, fragile or soft baitfish with thin skin won't stand up to wave action or nibbling as well as firmer fish or at least fish with a tough hide.

Any fish with heavy, hard scales that is to be used for chunk bait should first be scaled. Some experienced anglers also gut the fish. If it is a baitfish of small size, and fairly slender, it can be cut crosswise — steaked — through the backbone. These cross-section chunks are then attached to the hook not just through the soft middle-section meat, but by shoving a hook through the skin on one side, across through the flesh and out the skin on the other side. This assures that the bait will stay on the hook for casting and will stand firm against wave action. Sometimes a treble hook is used, and a chunk hooked with at least two of the hooks.

The other common method of cutting, when a larger fish is used or one that is thick or deep in the body, is to scale it and then slash off fillets. These can then be cut in meaty cross strips or chunks, wrapped around all three

Large baitfish can be filleted and scaled, then cross-cut strips or chunks used on single or treble hooks.

127

hooks of a treble, or doubled and hooked through both sides so that the skin is impaled twice and the meat somewhat protected inside.

While pier and boat fishing for several kinds of small game fish I've often taken a pinfish, small jack, or grunt—any variety fairly deep in the body—laid it flat and slit it along the back lengthwise, then again just above the ribs. Now chunks with skin on can be lifted and cut off in any shape you desire. Small, triangular pieces hooked midway down the long sides tend to leave a V-shaped tail end hanging off the hook. This looks appealing when the bait is crawled slowly along bottom by reeling.

Chunk-cut baits can be thick or thin. Small-mouthed spadefish, prodigious fighters and excellent eating, can be caught one after the other when they are inshore in spring hanging around piers or jetties, and ready for spawning, by using a $\frac{1}{8}$-inch cube of cut bait, skin on, pinned to a very small hook. Jigging chunk baits a bit on and near bottom adds to their effectiveness because fish see the motion.

For fish with very small mouths, cut small cubes from a scaled fillet and impale on small hook.

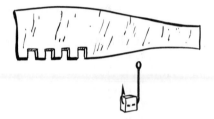

An old-hand salty fisherman I knew years ago in Florida always told me: "When in doubt or desperate, use a chunk cut from a fish—any fish—even the one you're fishing for. Something is sure to pick it up."

One caution regarding chunk-cut baits. When the meat of a fish is exposed to water, especially saltwater and particularly in currents or waves, the juices that give it its primary appeal and magnetic quality are soon leached away. It becomes pale and tasteless. So, don't endlessly dunk chunk baits. Change often. The blood and oil and scent of fresh chunks are what bring predators to investigate.

Strip baits. Strip bait means a strip of fish. But it is not all that simple. Cutting strips is a bit of an art. The basic idea behind the use of strip bait is to present a flexible section of fish so shaped by the cutter that in motion it will simulate something alive, presumably a living or crippled forage fish.

For that reason, strip baits are invariably given motion, chiefly by trolling them, but often by casting and reeling. In the surf strips are occasionally used, the teasing, living motion being produced by the undulations of the waves. Strips are also used at times wherever currents run. In an earlier reference to the use of ribbonfish as bait, I noted that this very compressed, slender fish, strung as a rule with two hooks, is let overside on some Texas offshore craft and allowed simply to drift off, sinking slowly and riding currents, meanwhile simulating a live or crippled forage fish because its superflexibility produces constant undulations. The ribbonfish is probably the one whole fish most comparable to strip bait.

Because a great many of the top marine game fish, from marlin to king mackerel, wahoo, dolphin, bluefish, striped bass, barracuda, and many others, even the groupers, are so addicted to a diet heavy in other fish, strip baits are extremely effective on them. Further, all these species, and numerous others, are trolled for, a method offering an opportunity to cover much water and thus present the bait over a broad expanse of water. Strip baits are mainstays of trolling anglers. In fact, they originally evolved long ago for trolling use for two reasons: a trolled strip usually has better action than a whole baitfish alive or dead; and it is a simple way to carry bait since there is no need to keep it alive.

It is a well-proven fact that strip baits are often far more productive even than live baitfish of a variety a given game species feeds on.

Needless to say, because of the great popularity of strip baits over many years, widely differing ways of cutting them have evolved from place to place. Thus the preparation of strip baits years ago came to be something of an art among the hard-core marine-fishing fraternity. Certainly anybody can fillet a baitfish, cut lengthwise strips of the fillets, hook them up and catch fish. But strip designs have evolved fitted to several purposes, and from place to place dozens of ideas and refinements have appeared. It would be nearly impossible to cover all of them, but some of the basic cuts and ideas are dealt with in the following material.

Like chunk-cut baits, strips exude oil and juices, thereby laying a kind of trail as they are pulled through the water. Also like chunks, exposure to water soon leaches away the oil and juice, and the scent. However, the flashing motion of a strip also appeals dramatically to game-fish vision, whereas chunk baits are ordinarily stillfished. Thus a strike on a well-used strip may occur simply because a predator races after it, attracted by the motion. It strikes impulsively to keep the bait from getting away. Nonetheless, fresh strips, especially at slow trolling speeds, outproduce those unduly "weathered," so it is a good idea to change the bait often.

Most baitfish used for strips are selected both for oily flesh and for tough skin. Mullet, mackerel, bonito, balao are good examples, although numerous others also serve. If a scaly fish is to be used, it should first be scaled. Meticulous strip fishermen then cut out the fins and slice off whole fillets on each side, leaving both head and tail as refuse attached to the backbone.

Baitfish to be strip cut, incidentally, should not have deteriorated at all. That is, they can be killed for cutting, or fresh-dead on ice, or even frozen. But the idea is to have the bait in such a condition that it will ooze out the proper fresh-smelling fluids.

After the fillets are ready, they are cut into lengthwise strips. For most medium to large game-fish trolling purposes, these should be from 1 to 1½ inches wide. The shape of any given strip at this stage doesn't matter much.

Preparation of strip baits is begun by slicing a scaled fillet lengthwise into strips about an inch wide.

Its final shape will be deftly designed by the angler's sharp knife. Obviously the final size of any strip bait must be suited to the intended quarry. I've used tiny ones only an inch long, or even less, casting them with spin tackle for mangrove snappers, small snook, and the myriad dwellers of some of the Everglades canals. Trolling for groupers in Florida waters, one skipper friend of mine always used strips about 4 or 5 inches long. That's the size many Pacific Coast fishermen offer to yellowtail and barracuda. For larger species, strips up to 8 or 10 inches or even a foot are usual on all coasts.

If any rib bones are left on the fillets, they should be carefully sliced away. A strip bait should be entirely boneless. In addition, it is not a good idea to cut a lot of baits at one time. Cutting them as needed assures freshness, although cutting a few and keeping them iced is all right. Never should strips be left out where they will begin to dry.

If the flesh on the thicker strips cut from a fillet seems too heavy, it should be thinned down appreciably. Some adept strip cutters not only thin the flesh side but with a very sharp, thin knife trim and feather the edges also, and the tail end. But that final trimming and smoothing is not done until the strip is cut to proper shape.

As noted, there are numerous differing ideas about shaping a strip. However, the basic design is to taper it from a wide, square head gently down to a thin, pointed tail. The flesh should be cut down very thin on the last inch (of a 5-inch strip, less on shorter ones) of the pointed tail end. This makes the tail exceedingly flexible. Some old hands claim the flesh should be sliced away entirely from the tail point, leaving only the skin, which will wriggle and flap as the strip is moved.

Then the head end gets attention. The consensus among strip-bait fishermen is that the most natural action is when a strip does not turn and twist. To insure that it rides flat, a slice is made at an angle backward across most of the squared head end. If this piece is cut away and the hook then placed through the small portion left as it was originally, the pull is straight down the long side of the strip, so that it tends to remain stable when in motion.

Most, but not all, strip fishermen run the hook through the flesh side first, and out through the skin. This does not always guarantee that the bait will ride skin side up or flesh side up, but it is the best hooking procedure.

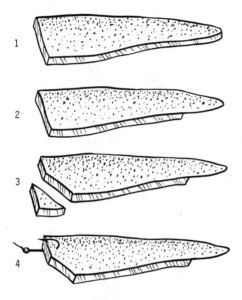

Steps in fashioning finished flat-r ding strip bait: (1) taper to narrow tail; (2) slice flesh away from tail skin so tail will flap; (3) slice head end at an angle; (4) place hook through portion of head still left.

There are occasions — or individual whims — that demand that a strip bait should not only flutter at modest speed, undulating over its thin length, but also gyrate slowly. Whenever the strip is cut and hooked so that it will turn, obviously a swivel must be used between leader and line to avoid line twist.

There are a number of cut designs to make a strip twist. Sometimes the edges are cut in an uneven pattern, a kind of zigzag up toward the head, so that one side is indented and the opposite one bulges outward. The hook placement is the important matter if you want the strip to turn. Usually the hook is run under the skin or through two very short crosswise slits in the skin up near the head, and the hook and line are pulled through. Then the hook point is run through the skin again, on one side of the strip near its edge, about a third of the way toward the tail. This insures that the bait will not run a flat course.

To cause a strip bait to spin or turn slowly, form edges in a zig-zag pattern, then run hook and line through skin slit, and hook the point through the side.

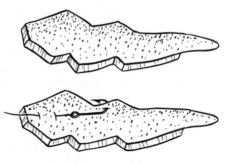

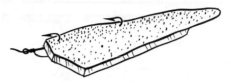

Two- or even three-hook rigs are favored by many strip trollers. Sketch shows how to place hooks of two-hook rig so strip rides level.

Speed of troll, or casting retrieve, will dictate how fast the strip turns. If you want to retrieve or move a boat very slowly, experiment with placing the hook point farther back toward the tail end. If the speed is to be fast, hook the strip nearer the head.

Two- and three-hook rigs are favored by a high percentage of strip-bait fishermen, at least with medium to large strips. Most use ready-made rigs obtainable in tackle shops, although it is easy enough to make up your own. The length of the strip dictates whether two or three hooks will hold the bait. Two-hook setups are the more common. On occasion the eye of one hook is slipped over the point and barb of another so that the tandem hooks are spaced a hook length apart. My personal preference is for snelling one hook to the other. This spaces the hooks farther apart and also makes a more limber rig.

Although trolling is the main method of strip-bait fishing, as I've said strips are extremely productive for all sorts of marine sport fish when cast. Even flounders are susceptible when strips are slowly bounced along bottom, and redfish (channel bass) on shallow bay grass flats and over shell beds can be driven forage-wild by properly fished strips that are thin and active. Thus the strip bait has a largely unexplored range of possibilities, and anglers who start to experiment more with casting tackle in inside waters may find themselves converts to strip fishing.

Possibly many readers have heard of "mooching" for salmon on the Pacific Coast and its tidal rivers. Old-time salmon fishermen may find fault with my description of mooching as simply a variation of jigging. But it is an exact one, and it can apply to strip-bait fishermen not only for salmon but for all manner of marine fish of bottom or near-bottom proclivities.

Stripped of mumbo-jumbo, mooching is basically a matter of letting a strip bait down to, or near, bottom, moving the boat ahead (or reeling in line, or drifting and intermittently pumping the rod) to raise the bait, then letting it slack again so that it sinks, then raising it again, and so on. This is a deadly tactic. But the point I wish to make is that the term "mooching" has long attached itself only to fishing for salmon in the Northwest, whereas the fundamental ideas or technique can be altogether as productive when used even in outside waters with large strips for big fish, or for the more stodgy denizens, such as flatfishes, of many an inshore or bay situation.

It is necessary to interject here that mooching for salmon is generally not done with a plain strip-cut bait but with what is known as a "plug cut." The head of a whole baitfish such as a small herring is cleanly cut off with a very

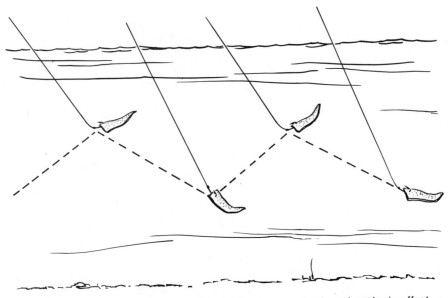

Here is the way a strip bait is "mooched." Boat moves slowly and angler in effect pumps the bait up and lets it out in a kind of jigging motion. Down-flutter is most appealing to most game fish.

sharp knife, on a slant, the cut running at an angle from the back downward and slightly rearward. The entrails are taken out. A two-hook rig is standard, with a couple of inches of line between hooks. One hook is run under the skin and through flesh near the top of the head end, out again and embedded through the back or else the side. The other hook is secured in the tail section. This plug of bait will now turn slowly when raised and let back. Whole baitfish, two-hook rigged, may be mooched also. The first hook is run from below up through the snout and secured into the body forward of the dorsal fin. The second one goes into the rear top, aft of the dorsal.

Much "mooching" is done with a plug-cut baitfish, shown here with hook placement. Actually plug-cutting is basically removal of head with a slanted, downward cut.

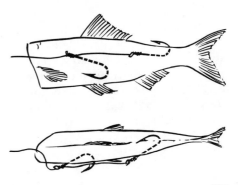

133

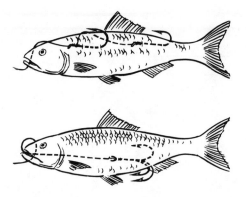

Whole baitfish, rigged with two hooks, may also be "mooched."

Strip baits can be designed for surface fishing and are extremely effective there for several kinds of fish. For a long time strip baits trolled on surface have been catching sails, marlin, dolphin, and any other open-water species that will come to the surface to feed. The method is also effective at times in bays, when the strip is cast and kept on surface. When channel bass feed over shallow flats, a strip retrieved on top will take them. The idea in all use of strip baits on surface is to keep them planing, sliding along so that if possible a good wake and a tail of spray result. Even at speeds that cause the bait to skip and alight over and over, it is effective, resembling a flying fish.

Anglers fish surface strips in different ways. Sometimes they are fished with tall outriggers, to help keep them on top. Wading and small-boat anglers use a long rod and lift it high as they reel, again forcing the bait to stay on surface. However, cutting and hooking a strip properly will assure that it planes. Obviously the trolling or reeling speed must be matched to the action of the bait, so that it can't sink.

The strip is cut with a perfectly squared-off head end. It is not tapered all the way from head to tail. An 8-inch strip, for instance, that is an inch wide, should be left as is at least two-thirds of the way toward the tail. From there on the tail section is abruptly tapered to a point. Most or all of the flesh is delicately sliced off from the tapered tail, so that it will flap as the strip moves.

Now the flesh at the head end of the strip is carefully thinned. The knife must be sharp and thin-bladed to make these strips properly. The flesh should be thinned for about 1 to 1½ inches back from the squared-off head. It is not all stripped from the skin but is sliced evenly so that the front end is about half as thick as the long middle section of the strip. Then, with the strip laid skin side down, this thin front end is rolled back. The hook is next thrust from the skin side up through the roll, and out again.

Some anglers use a two-hook rig. The two may be tied on short twin lengths of line to the same swivel. One hook holds the roll on the right side,

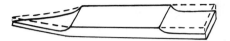

The three steps in fashioning a strip bait that is to ride flat on the surface.

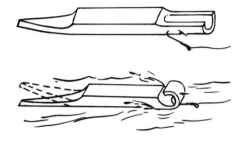

Some anglers use a two-hook rig of the type shown here to assure that the trolled strip rides as it should.

the other on the left. The use of two hooks insures that this rolled-back section of the strip stays that way, but one hook usually does the job almost as well. Thus arranged, when the strip is pulled along surface it is like a flat-bottomed bobsled with a curled-up front dash. The design keeps it planing, as long as there is speed enough so that it cannot sink. On both coasts and in the Gulf, surface strip-bait fishing is extremely productive.

Eels

Eels belong to the zoological family *Anguillidae*. They are actually true fishes but are covered here by themselves because they are in appearance so unlike other fishes. Their life history is complex. Eels spawn only in the sea but enter freshwater and travel immense distances. Their use as bait is almost entirely in saltwater. The common or American eel is the variety used. Long ago the eel became a standard bait along the New England coast and midway down the Atlantic Coast. Although it ranges far south, seldom does it find its way to the bait bucket anywhere but along the upper half of the United States Atlantic Coast.

Method of rigging eel that is fresh dead or frozen.

Live eels of moderate size are generally hooked through the tail and allowed to swim free. But the angler must keep them away from hiding places, which they will attempt to enter. Dead eels are sometimes preserved in brine. The entire eel is placed on the hook. Rigging is ordinarily accomplished with a needle. A piece of line or wire 12 to 15 inches long, attached to a hook, is threaded into the needle, passed into the eel from below near the vent, run forward and brought out the mouth. It is pulled snug enough so that the hook shank is up inside the body with the bend and point thrusting out from below, near or at the vent. The forward end of the piece of line (or wire) is run through the eye of a second hook and then bound to the shank. That hook is thrust from below the throat up through and out the top of the head behind the eye. A swivel is attached by a very short loop of line or wire to the eye of the head hook.

Rigged eels are trolled or cast, or even sometimes drifted. If live eels are used for trolling or casting the hook should pass through both lips, the lower lip only, or through the eyes. They are quite a tough bait, exceedingly tenacious of life. Although many fish species readily take eels, their main use along the Atlantic is for striped bass. This is in fact one of the prime offerings for this dynamic game fish. Bluefish also eagerly snap at eels. However, live eels are not practical because the blues slash them to pieces, usually without getting hooked. When fished for blues, dead eels must be used with wire or chain interior rigging, and preferably also with a wire leader.

If live eels are used, hook in one of the ways shown.

136

If you use a live eel bait for the first time, you'll find it exceedingly slippery—just like the old saying indicates. Gloves or an old towel to hold it with will help. Dead eels are a bit easier to handle. If you have ready access to eels for bait purposes, bear in mind that they are excellent bait for almost any bottom dweller when used as chunk bait. Simply cut crosswise. Eels also make unusually flexible, tough strip baits. Some East Coast anglers skin eels and rig the hide with hooks inside. This specialized approach, however, is more a lure than a bait technique.

To anyone new to saltwater the term "sand eel" is certain to be confusing, and a lot of moderately experienced marine anglers may well be confused by it. Many fishing books speak of using eels for bait and then apply to them the terms "eel" and "sand eel" interchangeably. Actually there is no such thing as a sand eel. The bait referred to, also a true fish, is a creature that superficially resembles an eel but belongs to another family, the *Ammodytidae*. Its correct name is the sand lance (sometimes spelled "launce"), but undoubtedly the colloquial "sand eel" will persist. Some less than observant fishermen seem to believe this is the young of the common eel.

There are three species of sand lances, all of them resident on the Atlantic, one also found along portions of the Pacific. Typically their range is northern. Utilized only occasionally on the Pacific, they are a rather common bait along the upper part of the Atlantic Coast. The sand lance is often very abundant in the surf along sandy shores, where it burrows into the soft sand with great agility. Sand-lance schools now and then swarm in shallow water and can be dipped up. They are also dug from sand and sometimes thrown in abundance by waves onto sandy beaches.

At maximum the sand lance grows to only about 7 inches. On the average it is smaller, perhaps 4. It is easy to distinguish between the lance and a true eel. Eels have a continuous dorsal fin that runs along much of the back, on around the tail and becomes an anal fin without any break. The sand lance has a long dorsal that ends before the tail. The tail is a standard forked caudal fin, which is separated from the anal fin.

The sand lance is a fine bait, alive or fresh-dead or even frozen. Used with a surf rig that utilizes a submerged float to keep the lance from burrowing in sand, it is productive, taking various surf dwellers. It is also fine bait for almost any other fish to which it can be presented.

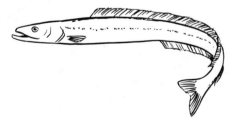

The "sand eel" is actually a fish, the sand launce, a prime bait.

Crustaceans

The crustaceans literally wear their skeletons on the outside. There are many species, and among them are numerous quite different creatures. But they are alike in having no backbone and in having jointed bodies, jointed legs, and jointed antennae, and a "crust," or tough outside covering of a substance called chitin that gives rigidity and protection, and to which the muscles are attached inside.

This large zoological classification contains the lobsters, both the claw lobster of New England and the spiny lobster or saltwater crayfish found along both coasts. It should be noted that lobsters make excellent fish bait. However, with their present-day standing as high-priced and gourmet "people bait," it's doubtful if any ever find their way to a hook. The crustaceans with which marine anglers are concerned in the bait category are the shrimps, crabs, and sand fleas or sandbugs. Barnacles are also among the crustaceans, even though they appear superficially more like mollusks. Although they can be chipped or spudded from pilings as a kind of chum, barnacles are not important as a bait crustacean.

Shrimp. Throughout all inside and near-shore waters of the Atlantic and the Gulf the shrimp is probably the most important of all baits. It is even used to some extent in offshore blue water. It can be truly said that there is no predaceous saltwater fish that will not take a shrimp-baited hook. On the Pacific Coast shrimp were slow starters as bait, and still today they are not as massively used there as in the Gulf and along the Atlantic Coast. Part of this is due to the fewer readily available shrimp species along Pacific shores.

There are many varieties of shrimp. Most of the larger-sized ones used both as bait and for human consumption come from the southern Atlantic area and the Gulf. The species involved are the brown shrimp, the white shrimp, and the pink shrimp. Rock shrimp are seldom available, although they are abundant in numerous locations. They have a very hard shell and are much like diminutive lobsters. They are superb table fare, and just as excellent for bait use, particularly when peeled. However, the commercial shrimp fishery has to date been unable to establish more than a minor market for them for human consumption, and so fishermen seldom see this shrimp, and many people do not even know it exists. As this is written there is some experimentation along the Texas coast with commercializing rock shrimp.

Along the Pacific several varieties of shrimp are available. The ghost shrimp lives in burrows in the mud of shallow bays and is usually sold in bait shops as "saltwater crayfish." Fished in the surf, or for bay fish, or along rocks and from piers, ghost shrimp catch practically any fish to which they are presented. Another Pacific shrimp used as bait is the red rock shrimp. Its body length is about 3 inches. This is a species with a rather hard carapace, but it is readily taken by rockfish and most bottom dwellers, and it is also a good surf bait.

Anyone who intends to catch his own shrimp for bait, by trawl or trap, should be aware that fishing laws must be consulted. There may be size limits, seasons, regulations on legal methods even down to the size of traps, and also in some places bag limits by poundage. Few fishermen, however, catch their own. Bait shrimp are available, alive or frozen, almost everywhere along our coasts, even on occasion in supermarkets.

Shrimp can be fished successfully in almost every conceivable fashion. I have touched on some of the methods at various places earlier in this book. Live shrimp can be stillfished beneath a cork. They can be cast and retrieved slowly. A highly sporting way to use good-sized shrimp for kingfish (king mackerel) and school dolphin offshore is to locate a school, then employ fairly light spinning or bait-casting tackle, about the same as for bass in freshwater. No weight, or only a small clinch-type sinker, gives the bait free rein and allows it to sink naturally while kicking in a lively manner. This is often called "free-shrimping."

Casting live shrimp with whippy tackle in bays, for speckled trout or other fish, I have already mentioned earlier. Live shrimp are also deadly in the surf, or when fished on bottom with a sinker at the end of the line and a dropper up a bit to keep the shrimp from hiding and to discourage crabs and nibblers. Drifting a shrimp down a tidal current, especially if you toss out a few for chum to draw and hold moving fish, is most productive.

The so-called popping cork has been mentioned several times. To review it briefly, this method is a favorite of wading or boat fishermen in southern bays of the Atlantic and the Gulf, for speckled trout (weakfish). (See under "Saltwater Rigs" for instructions on how to make the setup.) A live shrimp is fished a couple of feet as a rule below the dish-faced popping cork. Trout feeding on grass shrimp or other forage often swirl near surface, leaving a boil and sometimes making a slurping sound. The cast is made, and on the slow retrieve the cork is jerked every couple of feet. This makes a roil and a surface sound, both easily seen and heard by the fish. Below the cork the shrimp dances as the cork is popped. The combination is irresistible. Usually, but not always, live shrimp must be used. Dead shrimp are often turned down by the feeding fish.

There are several ways of hooking live shrimp. The hook-up most commonly employed for all fish that will be inclined to engulf the bait at one gulp is through the head. Care must be taken not to kill the shrimp. Hold one up to the light and you will see a dark area inside the head back from the snout. Avoid this vital spot. Some anglers run the hook from side to side through the head just behind the snout. Others hook from underneath, upward, bringing the barb well out of the carapace. The late George Clark of Port Aransas, Texas, taught me years back to use a treble hook of modest size when fishing live shrimp with a popping cork, or when casting

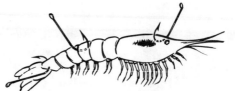

Various ways of placing shrimp on a hook. Note dark spot inside the head back of snout; piercing it will kill the shrimp.

them without cork or weight for trout. The mouth of a weakfish tears easily, and a treble gets a better bite.

The shrimp can also be hooked from below through the last body segment just ahead of the tail flippers. There are those who believe in threading the first several tail segments onto the hook. Some bring the point out below, some above. There are also devotees of running the hook under a mid-segment of the back. In my estimation this is a poor arrangement. I have seen anglers use the tail-threading method but pinch off the flippers before doing so. They claim this keeps the bait from turning when it is reeled along. However, my own opinion is that tail threading is not a sound idea, except possibly for bottom feeders. The shrimp does not look lifelike. The best approaches are to hook it through the head, or through the last tail segment.

Along the upper Atlantic Coast, in locations for example along the New Jersey coast, old hands bait with small grass shrimp, as they are called, using two or even three on a hook. Chumming with more of the same, they drift the baits down the current of an inlet after weakfish and striped bass.

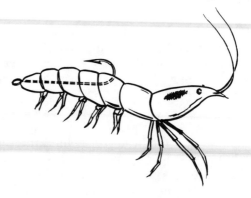

Some anglers tail-hook the shrimp but pinch off the flippers first. They claim this keeps the shrimp from turning as it is reeled along.

In instances such as these, the shrimp are simply impaled anyhow. They don't need to be alive and kicking. When fish are eagerly into the chum the bait doesn't have much time to kick anyway.

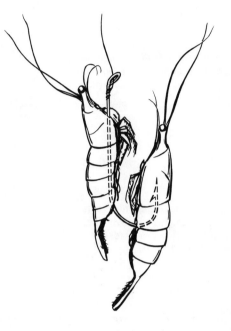

Along the upper Atlantic coast the small grass shrimp is a prime bait. Many fishermen use more than one on a hook.

Ordinarily dead shrimp are not fished whole. Watch the pier fishermen, who use hundreds of pounds of frozen shrimp. The experienced ones twist off the head and toss it over for chum. Frozen, shrimp are never quite as firm and tough as live or fresh-dead ones. Most fish species that readily seize dead shrimp, particularly after they've been frozen, pull off the head end without getting hooked. Thus most anglers use only the tail of bait shrimp of the packaged frozen type. It is simply threaded on the hook. You can take your choice, threading from the large end back to the flippers, or vice versa. It really makes little difference. It's a good idea to pull off the legs, for this discourages bait stealers.

Large fresh-dead shrimp tails, peeled, are a killer for channel bass feeding in the shallow water of grass flats and over shell beds in bays. Wading anglers in my region thread on a big, freshly peeled tail and cast it like a lure. The technique is to spot, with polaroids, a pod of foraging reds. They move slowly along, but are awesomely skittish in water 1 or 2 feet deep. The tail is cast past and ahead of feeding fish. A lone one is less easily spooked than a group. The rod is held high and the shrimp tail reeled back right along the surface, so that it leaves a small wake. When a big bull red slams it in water that thin, the battle is violently explosive and the angler lucky if he isn't cut off on shells.

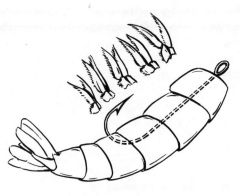

Frozen shrimp tails are hooked as shown. It's a good idea to pull off the legs to keep nibblers from pulling on them.

Large fresh-dead shrimp tails, peeled and cast as a lure over shallow grass flats, are deadly for channel bass (redfish).

For a myriad pan-sized marine fishes, small bits of shrimp tail work wonders, or the whole tails of small shrimp can be threaded on. To repeat, there is probably no predator saltwater fish that cannot be caught with a shrimp. It is the one bait of which it may be said: "Whenever in doubt or difficulty, try it."

Over recent years, incidentally, shrimp have become quite popular in some areas for fishing in freshwater. For example, along the upper Gulf Coast of Florida where large rivers empty into bays and the Gulf, there are expanses of brackish water where, as salinity decreases inland, both freshwater and saltwater fish consort. Largemouth black bass seize a shrimp here as avidly as any redfish or speckled trout.

The use of shrimp is carried much further, however, up into wholly freshwater stretches. Whole shrimp and shrimp tails are fished for bass, large sunfishes, and catfish. Further, far inland it is quite common nowadays to discover packaged frozen bait shrimp even in supermarkets. It is a prime bass and catfish bait. An interesting switch is the use of freshwater crayfish, relatives of the shrimp, in saltwater. Along the Oregon coast, for example, some anglers swear by the effectiveness of crayfish or crayfish tails for numerous saltwater species.

Crabs. Several saltwater game fish are partial to crabs. The cobia, called ling in some places, is also known as a "crab-eater" in others. The permit,

142

considered a very prize catch in Florida, feeds extensively on crabs. Bonefish, tarpon, bluefish, striped bass, weakfish, channel bass, croakers, tautog, sheepshead, the corbina, lingcod, and carbezon of the Pacific, the flatfishes, groupers, and a number of others eat crabs of several kinds.

Some large fish, such as tarpon, scoop up whole adult blue crabs at a quick bite. Channel bass or redfish prefer crabs of half dollar size or smaller. The same is true of the permit. Sheepsheads, with their small mouths filled with paved teeth, delight in gobbling small fiddler crabs not much bigger than a dime. In fact, they are so handy at cutting one from a hook that at times they clean off the bait—snipping away with those sharp, broad teeth—without causing the slightest tremor of the line.

Crabs are a rather specialized bait, yet wherever they are handily available, on all our coasts, they are a prime forage of many fish, especially inshore, surf, and bay species, which grub them from sand and from among rocks and seaweed. It is not mandatory that an angler learn to identify numerous species of crabs. It is necessary to check laws regarding the taking of the large crabs used commercially for their meat. Most of the crabs one buys in bait shops or gathers along beaches or on tidal flats are not eating varieties. Moreover, it is the small crabs that make up most of the bait picture.

Probably the most common bait crab is the fiddler. These small crabs burrow in salt marshes and sandy beaches, form huge colonies, are sold in bait shops and are also easily gathered on the spot, even though they run rather fast, and sideways. The male has a single large claw. It should be broken off before the crab is put on the hook. Sand, or ghost, crabs are found on the warmer portions of all our coasts. They prefer much drier sand than the fiddler, and many specimens are much larger.

One of the most common bait crabs is the small fiddler. The large single claw of the male should be broken off before baiting.

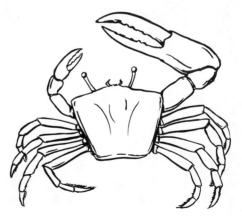

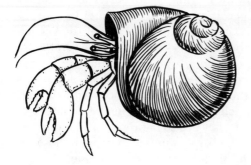

The hermit crab lives in a cast-off mollusk shell, has a soft, long abdomen. It is an excellent, easily-hooked bait.

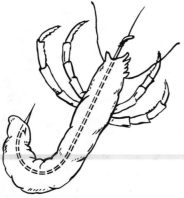

The hermit crab is extracted from its borrowed mollusk-shell home and hooked as shown.

Another important bait crab is the hermit crab. Although there are species of hermit crabs on both the Atlantic and Pacific, it is along the southern Atlantic and portions of the Gulf Coast that the hermit crab is most popular for bait. This interesting crab is found in tidal pools and shallows. It has a long, soft abdomen with a hooklike tail. Because the soft body portion is extremely vulnerable, it lives in the empty shells of snails,

144

whelks, conches, and other mollusks, extending its claw to drag its home around with it. As it outgrows one home, it leaves and finds a larger one.

Hermit crabs can be removed from their adopted homes by applying heat, or cracking the shell. I have pulled big ones out with pliers. Small hermit crabs, because of their soft lower body, are easily threaded on a hook. This is a great advantage, and moreover that soft abdomen is what makes them such prime bait. I have used cut chunks of hermit crabs very successfully, too. Large hermits, for presentation to big fish, can be hooked through the hard part of the back, or collar. The hook is thrust down through the body to protrude between the legs.

Small rock crabs of several kinds and green crabs are old stand-bys along the Atlantic, especially the northern half. Kelp crabs, other rock crabs, and the so-called shore crabs serve West Coast anglers. Most of these are fished in small sizes. Rock crabs of half dollar size occasionally mop up channel bass, either in bays or in the surf. The large crabs, such as adult blue crabs, have long been extremely popular with East Coast anglers from Chesapeake Bay northward. They are preferred in the shedder or soft-shelled stage. However, the popularity of large crabs for commercial food consumption, heavy fishing for them, and the price of them plus laws pertaining to taking them have all to some extent inhibited the use of big crabs for bait purposes.

There are no special rigs for fishing crabs. The bait can be used on almost any saltwater rig. But hooking crabs is always something of a problem. Fiddlers can be hooked by piercing the abdomen and bringing the hook clear through and out the back. However, the process often splits the crab, and it won't stay on the hook. Some old hands pull off a leg and shove the hook gingerly into the opening that is left, then carefully push only the point out through the back.

Half dollar- to silver dollar-sized rock and green crabs, or others with hard shells, are handled in several different ways. The back of the crab can be removed carefully. This allows juices to flow and also eliminates a fish tearing at the bait to avoid the hard cover. Large crabs are sometimes mashed across the back before placement on the hook, to more quickly attract action. Whether this is done or not the hook can be thrust through one side of the shell from below (this would be the point area on blue crabs), or it can be thrust from below up through the shell between the rear flippers, or crosswise through the body from side to side beneath the back.

There is no difficulty in hooking crabs in their soft-shelled stages. Whole large shedders are hooked as a rule through the rear portion of the soft shell. All crabs should have the large pinchers removed before they are put on the hook. Commonly the pinchers of fiddlers or other small crabs are tossed over as chum. All told, crabs are fine bait for a wide variety of marine game fish. The fundamental problems with them are that in the

There are numerous varieties of small rock crabs and other kinds. All serve well.

Large crabs, such as the adult blue crab, especially in the shedder stage, are much used along the Atlantic and the western Gulf. Tarpon, stripers, cobia, and other big game fish eagerly seize them.

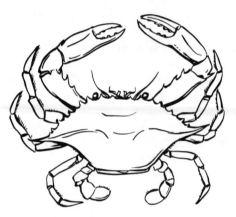

hard stages they are difficult to hook properly, and that if you try to remove the hard shell and just use the meat, placing it on a hook securely is not always easy. Crabs broken up and used as chum, even if you then fish with other bait, are most provocative in tolling in game fish.

Sand Fleas. The mole crabs, as they are often called, are relatives of the crabs. So many names are used for them and their close relatives that a few must be noted here: sand flea, sandbug, sand crab, scud. Technically there is confusion here. The small creature in question is not a scud, and it is certainly not a "bug" or "flea." It is a true crustacean. I knew them years ago as "sand fleas" on one stretch of Pacific beach, and by the same name in Florida.

There are several varieties on both coasts. They are about an inch long at full growth, have a hard, oval calapace and two long, plumed antennae.

All crabs should have claws removed previous to use as bait. Some hooking methods are also shown here, the lower of the three sketches showing how to hook fiddler crab by thrusting hook point in hole where big claw has been removed.

They burrow in sand at the edge of the surf, are tossed in and out by waves and move with the tides. This generation of anglers probably never knew it, but there was a time many years ago when two highly renowned ichthyologists stated flatly that the pompano could not be caught with hook and line. Later it was discovered that here and there an old Florida coastal cracker had long been catching them, using a sand flea for bait.

But that's only part of the story. The claim was made quite seriously by writers of that day — it had been told them deadpan by the salty characters involved — that the way it was done was to put a sand flea on a hook and

Mole crabs, found on all coasts, are sometimes called sand fleas or sand bugs. They make excellent bait.

make a cast from the beach out into the surf at an angle to the left. After reeling in very slowly, you were to move down the beach to your left and make a second cast to your right, crossing where the other had been. Then you again reeled in slowly, intersecting the path of the first retrieve. After that you cast precisely to the intersection and let the sand-flea bait lie. Pompano would follow the trails to the intersection — and *whammo!*

Well, it's a good tale, possibly with guile attached. And the fact is that this little surfside crustacean has long been the most effective bait for the often hard-to-catch pompano. It also catches all other fish that frequent the surf. That is where almost all anglers acquainted with it use it. Along the Pacific it regularly mesmerizes the popular corbina and the several just as popular croakers, as well as a number of the husky surf perches. Around Florida and along portions of the Atlantic, channel bass, sheepsheads, whiting, weakfish, and all varieties that visit the surf snap up this bait.

The sand flea is usually hooked from the rear and beneath, up through the body, with the hook coming out at the rear of the back. Another hooking method is to thrust the hook in between the antennae, bend and point down, and thread the creature on so that the hook comes out at the rear end with the bend and point on the underside.

Several surf rigs are employed with this bait. If the bait is threaded on, obviously it is dead or almost dead and cannot burrow into the sand. If it is hooked through the rear so that it stays alive, then sometimes it is used with a spreader rig, with each dropper leader carrying a small float. These keep the bugs above the sand and allow them to move enticingly to the wave action.

148

Mollusks

The variety of mollusks along all United States coasts is practically infinite. Some fish species are equipped with crusher teeth purposely to enable them to feed on these shelled creatures. The tautog, a favorite of fishermen from Cape Cod to the Carolinas, is often called an "oysterfish." Mollusks are one of the most important items of its diet, and the powerful crusher teeth easily break up the shells. The drums, the sheepshead, and a number of other species heavily utilize mollusks, shells and all.

All inshore and surfline, inlet, and bay fishes eat mollusk meat whenever they have the opportunity, whether or not they are equipped to crush shells. Many a univalve mollusk, when protruding from its shell to feed or in the case of the bivalves such as clams with the shell opened somewhat and the living creature extended, are snapped at by any fish that is able to sidle up quietly or is quick enough to slash off a piece before the creature can retreat.

Bivalve and univalve mollusks. In Florida I used to pick up small conches that had been pushed ashore by a storm, or else pick them from bottom in a shallow tidal flat. A few minutes' exposure to fresh or hot water soon forced the weakening animal to extend its tough "foot." Then I could pull the whole creature out of the shell with pliers. A cross section of the tough muscle, with some of the soft meat adhering, made an excellent bait.

Probably the mollusks most famous as bait are the clams and mussels. Mussels are easily gathered from pilings and rocks along coasts as widely separated as Maine and California. Mollusk meat taken from the shell is used almost entirely within inside waters or along the surf or rocky beaches, and from piers and jetties. Any surf-frequenting fish will eagerly accept this bait. The same is true of bay fishes and of all those that dwell around or among rocks or on bottom.

The basic problem in fishing the mollusks is keeping a bait on the hook. Only a few parts of a mollusk are tough enough to stay on well, and these parts, among small mollusks, are often too small to use for good-sized game

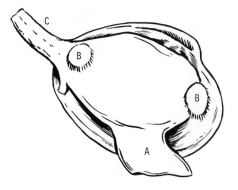

Several parts of a mollusk are tough enough to stay on a hook. The so-called foot (A) of all mollusks is one part. The adductor muscles (B) of the bivalve mollusks, which open and close the shell, also serve. The siphons of some species (C) also hook well.

fish. In bivalve mollusks—those with two halves of shell that open, i.e., clams, oysters, scallops—the adductor muscles (there are either one or two) are among the tough parts. These are the buttons of strong muscle that attach the creature to its shell most solidly and do the opening and closing of it. The scallop you eat is that muscle.

Among such mollusks as large clams or the univalves like the conches and whelks, the foot is large enough so that it can be used as a bait, or in some cases cut into several baits. The so-called foot is the large, strong muscle, capable of much extension and contraction, by which the animal is able to move itself from place to place. The foot is extended from the shell, thrust forward and anchored solidly in mud or sand. As it contracts, the creature and its shell are pulled along. Probably everyone has seen mollusk tracks on shallow bottoms.

The siphons of the bivalves particularly are often tough enough, and in some varieties large enough, for bait. These are the muscular tubes that are extended from the shell (and of course can be withdrawn), through which the animal feeds. Plankton-filled water is brought in through one siphon and expelled through the other. Soft-shell or steamer clams, for example, have a long neck containing the siphons. These, and the siphons from

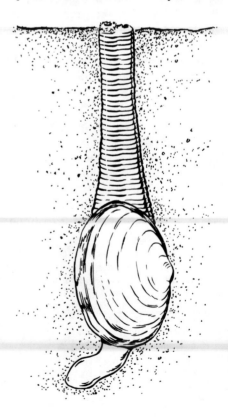

Clams such as the softshell have a long neck that encloses the siphons. Many anglers favor these as bait because they stay on a hook.

quahog clams on the East Coast and such varieties as the large and delicious Pismo clam on the Pacific, make a good bait tough enough to stay on the hook.

It must be noted that regulations for taking pertain to many mollusk varieties along our coasts. As an example, the Pismo clam in California has a size and bag limit. Mussels there become highly toxic during hot months — and elsewhere also at times — and it is then illegal, for one's own protection, to take them for human consumption. Abalone fishing is highly regulated. Thus, wherever you are, be sure what laws relate to any mollusk variety you wish to use for bait.

Among those who habitually fish mollusks as bait, there are differences of opinion about which parts serve best. Some California anglers save the siphons of Pismo and other large clams, believing they are best. Others use a chunk of the foot and still others pieces of the gut. If you open a good-sized clam shell and study the animal inside, you can easily see the various parts — foot, gut, siphons, etc.

If you like raw oysters, or at least are familiar with what they look and feel like, you quickly realize that putting a whole one on a hook is simple enough, but casting it would be all but certain to throw it off the hook. Even if it is let down for bottom stillfishing it may not last long against wave or current action and can be torn off easily by the smallest bait stealer.

Yet mollusk meat and whole mollusks of fair size have always been recognized as such excellent bait that anglers have devised endless schemes to try to lick the problems. Once in Florida, remembering my earlier experience with salted minnows for yellow perch in freshwater, I tried removing various mollusks whole from their shells and placing them on a layer of rock salt, then covering this with another layer of mollusks, and so on, in an earthen crock. This toughened them appreciably after a brief period. I then tested them on several kinds of pan-sized fish such as mangrove snappers, grunts, Bermuda chubs, and yellowtail snappers. Although I made no long tests, the fishing I did do with the salted meat was successful.

West Coast fishermen occasionally use sugar to toughen the meat. Some others have tried smoking and also simply partial drying. If you have ever eaten steamed clams you know that they have a fair amount of body and chewiness. Steamed mussels and clams are now and then fished and are apparently about as proficient in fish catching as the wholly raw article.

Anglers have also run up a number of ingenious rigging methods to try to lick the problem of holding soft, raw mollusk on a hook. The following are a few I have either tried or seen tried that work fairly well. A whole mollusk scooped from the shell, especially the bivalves such as mussels and clams, can be secured exactly like a gob of salmon roe. The line is run through the eye of the hook, preferably a bait-holder type. It is snelled to the hook well down toward where the bend begins. On a bait-holder hook, wrap and make the snell below the bait-holder barb on the shank, or if

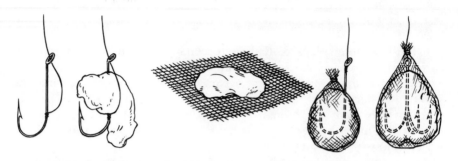

Methods of holding soft mollusk meat on hook: by a loop formed by snell to hook shank; by placing in net bag, as with salmon-egg slice.

there are two barbs, below the lower one. Now place the whole mollusk, or a portion of the meat, inside the loop formed by the line and the hook shank. Snug the line gently, leaving enough meat inside the hook bend so that it can be looped over the hook point and barb. This method holds fairly well if you are easy with it.

Some anglers use fine-mesh bags such as those also used for a cluster of salmon eggs or a gob of roe. The soft and juicy mollusk meat with a hook — single or treble — in it can be placed inside the small-mesh bag, with the bag secured to the hook shank or else to the line immediately above the hook eye. It is simply tied on with monofil. An advantage is that the mesh discourages small bait stealers. One school dislikes the idea of enclosing the mollusk meat, believing that some shy fish will turn it down unless it is out in the open.

Note well that one of the advantageous features of mollusks — especially whole ones or big gobs — as bait is that the juice, with or without a mesh bag, oozes out into the water and is an excellent attractor. In fact, ground or shredded clams and mussels or any other mollusks make excellent chum. This chum is much used along the upper Atlantic Coast but not seen as much elsewhere. Southern fishermen who are willing to take the time to collect and chop up any of the abundant mollusks easily accessible there can most successfully employ them to chum up and help hold almost any game fish.

Another method of securing mollusk bait to the hook is to twist a length of fine wire snugly to a hook shank, so that two ends as much as a couple of inches long thrust out from either side of the shank. Push the hook into the meat and lay the rest up the hook shank. Twist the wire several times around throughout the length of the bait. Monofil can serve instead of wire, but the fine wire is easier to twist, and to untwist for rebaiting.

Occasionally one sees a mollusk-meat rig made by stringing a bead on a line, then running the line through the eye of the hook. Then the end is run back through the bead and tied to the main line a couple of inches above the hook eye with a nonslip knot. This in effect leaves a loop with a bead on it above the hook. The bait is slipped into the loop and snugged down with the bead. Use a hook with an extra-short shank. The bait should be big enough so that it can be placed unevenly in the loop. The long end is then moved around so that the hook can be buried in it. Even this setup, like the loop on the hook shank, has to be handled gingerly to avoid throwing off the bait, even though the grip is quite solid.

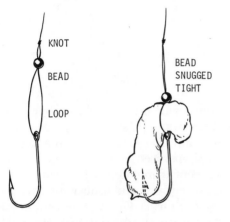

Another method of hooking mollusk meat is to make a small loop in the line above the hook, with a bead strung on it, and snug the bait into the loop. Impale the remainder over the point of the hook.

Aside from the above suggestions, and the use of the tough parts of mollusks as bait that can be cast, there are no special rigs for this bait. The fish finder, the standard surf rig, any stillfishing or bottom rig including a spreader all work fine. On jetties and along rocky coasts a gob of mollusk dropped into a crevice or a hole among rocks is certain to be snatched up quickly. If you can find a way to get the mollusk bait to the quarry without having it leave the hook, you can intrigue any species from a big striper or channel bass to a weakfish, sea bass, or croaker to the rockfishes and surf perches along the Pacific Coast.

Squid. Even though squids don't look like it, they are mollusks. The "shell" is a rather soft plate or "pen" within the body. The outer covering or mantle is formed of tough muscle. The tentacles at the head seize small fish and the sharp, horny beak in the mouth dismembers them. Squids are abundant along all our coasts. They usually move in large schools. They are literally jet propelled, squirting a stream of water that sends them swiftly swimming backward. When disturbed they emit a cloud of "ink" that surrounds them and in which they are able to hide or escape.

Some squids are large, but the average size is about 8 inches. They are heavily preyed upon by all predaceous saltwater fish and therefore are an excellent bait. Squids are also marketed for human consumption. Some

The squid is actually a mollusk whose tough flesh is a popular and extremely productive bait. Whole or cut squid are used.

people are extremely fond of them, but many others find the appearance and the slippery body totally repugnant to the palate.

The bait industry on both coasts nets and packages squid by the ton, and they are available in almost all bait shops, iced whole, frozen, and occasionally alive. I have purchased boxes of frozen chunk-cut squid on the Texas coast. There has long been an extensive squid fishery for both bait and human consumption at Monterey, California. Once, while salmon fishing there, I saw a squid boat lifting huge quantities of fresh-caught squid in a dump net up from the craft to a big truck on the dock. When the truck was loaded there were 15,000 pounds of squid aboard—and suddenly the enormous container split open. The whole slippery mass flooded out onto the dock! The few fishermen on the dock were told to help themselves. The clean-up job appeared awesome.

On the Pacific Coast squid are sometimes kept alive and fished for such species as yellowtail, big white sea bass, and lingcod (greenling). All of the rockfishes of the Pacific also eagerly gobble up squid, but for those species, and most others, the squid is cut into chunks. On the Atlantic and in the Gulf whole squid are trolled for any of the large pelagic game fish such as marlin, swordfish, and tuna. Black drum, cod, pollock, striped bass, flounders, and in fact practically any hungry fish will avidly seize cut-squid baits.

One of the important advantages of squid is that the muscle is very tough. Whole or cut up, it stays on a hook very well. I have seen several large black drum taken on the same chunk of squid, and still it clung to the hook so well that it had to be cut off to replace it with a fresh piece.

The best way to rig a whole fresh-dead or frozen squid for trolling is with two hooks in tandem. The lower hook is thrust crosswise through the head, sometimes through the eyes. The leader is then run through the body lengthwise, with a bait-threading needle, and brought out the rear. The second hook is firmly placed in the rear portion of the body, the leader run

Whole fresh-dead or frozen squid (above) are actually hooked tandem. The head of a squid (left), with tenacles and hooked crosswise through the eyes, is one of the best chunk baits for a wide variety of game fish.

through the hook eye and pulled barely snug. Then the tie is made. This setup keeps the bait stretched out in a natural stance, and moving backward, as it would if alive. Whole squid rigged thus are also cast and retrieved. A few fast turns of the reel, then a pause or short jerk, make the squid swim and drop back over and over. This is an appealing movement. If you lack a threading tool, simply run the leader material between the two hooks along the outside of the body.

Live squids are hooked through the rear part of the body. The hook should be shoved well inside the body with the barb coming out the side. Any portion of squid chunk-cut makes a fine and productive bait. However, a number of anglers believe the head, with its attached tentacles or arms (there are ten), is the best portion. Hooking it crosswise through the eyes places it solidly. For hooks and fish of modest size, squid tentacles are a prime bait. I have often sliced whole squid lengthwise, making thick strips from the body muscle, and used these as a bait to be cast and retrieved. This is much the same in action as the pork rind so common in freshwater fishing. Pieces of squid are especially suited to bottom fishing, because the muscle is so tough that small nibblers can seldom tear it apart.

Chunks of squid make an exceptional bait for surf fishing. The wave and casting action do not easily deteriorate the bait, and almost any fish of the surf, on any coast, can be caught on it. There are no special rigs involved for using squid. Bottom fishing, stillfishing with a bobber, using a spreader, a fish-finder rig—all present this bait properly in one or another marine habitat.

Marine worms. Worms of the sea coast are relatives of the angleworms, or annelids. There are hundreds of species. A few of these large enough to be suitable have long been used as one of the top baits for a wide variety of fish. Although they are seldom seen in the bait shops of our southern Atlantic and Gulf coasts, they are much used along the northern half of the

Marine worms are among the most popular of all inshore and bay baits on most of the Pacific and the upper half of the Atlantic coasts. This is one of the most common, the clamworm, or sandworm.

Atlantic Coast and almost everywhere on the Pacific. The marine-worm bait industry from New England to Long Island and on the California coast is truly big business.

There are two kinds of worms, with numerous species for each, that furnish the bulk of this bait. These are the clamworms, which are often called sandworms, and the bloodworms. Clamworms are abundant on both coasts, on the Atlantic chiefly over the northern waters but extending to the Carolinas, on the Pacific from Alaska to Mexico. They grow to as much as several feet long, but it is worms of 6 to 8 inches up to a foot in length that are sold for bait. Or an angler who is familiar with his territory can dig his own.

Clam- or sandworms live in burrows in sand or mud, among rocks and under them, among mussel colonies on pilings. Clammers digging in the mud flats of protected bays often uncover them. These worms are segmented, with a flattened body shape and fringed or bristly appendages along the body. Their horny jaws can give a painful nip to an angler careless in handling them. Colloquial names for the clamworm are heard in various places, usually related to the sort of habitat from which the worms were collected — mud worm, pile worm, rock worm, mussel worm.

Bloodworms occupy much the same habitats as the clamworms, although the latter as a rule are found in deeper burrows, and bloodworms prefer mud that is fairly firm. The range on both coasts is similar. The name "bloodworm" arose from the color of the juices in the body, which are often as red as human blood. The bloodworm to some extent resembles the earthworm. Its body is round and quite smooth, but with a fringe of very short appendages. The bloodworm also can inflict a nasty bite, and in some persons the pain and swelling caused by it are severe. In places this worm is called snout or proboscis worm. The rather blunt snout, which is employed in making the burrow, can be extended at will.

Tube worms, or parchment worms, are sometimes used for bait, mostly along the Pacific. These worms live in a U-shaped parchmentlike case, in

Bloodworms are found in most of the same places as the clamworms, and are as popular and effective.

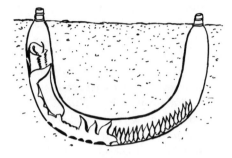

Parchment or tube worms are used to for bait on the Pacific coast.

masses on pilings or in mud flats. They make productive bait for a variety of surf perch and for the rockfishes and other Pacific varieties. They are gathered in their tubes and squeezed out to be threaded on the hook. Numerous other marine worms are used here and there. However the important kinds are the clamworms and bloodworms.

A broad variety of game fish avidly take them. I recall fishing years ago from a small rented boat along the Sound in populous Westchester County, New York, only a few miles from downtown New York City. It was my first experience with clamworms. We stillfished near a busy highway, tossing out the baited hook and letting it simply lie on bottom until we had a bite. The catch of small flounders we took was substantial. This was my first experience with this bait, and I didn't much like handling them. In addition, I received numerous nips on the fingers before I learned how to thread them defensively.

Fishing marine worms is very similar to using night crawlers in freshwater. For some fish species whole worms are threaded on a long-shanked

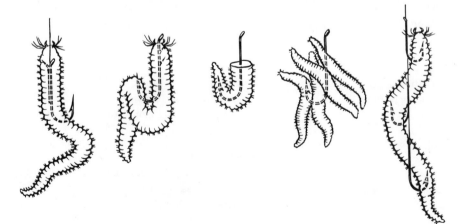

Methods of hooking marine worms.

157

hook, usually from the head end. The hook in some instances is brought out the side partway down, then the remainder of the worm is hooked on to make a U-shaped bait with a trailing tail. Pieces of worms are used for a myriad bottom fish such as flounders, porgies, and pan-sized varieties.

For large fish such as striped bass, channel bass, weakfish, black sea bass, the large croakers of the Pacific, halibut, and large flounders, whole sea worms are stretched out on either a tandem or a three-hook rig, exactly like night-crawler harnesses in freshwater. Often a spinner is included in the rig, or else the worm is trailed behind a spoon. The rig is cast and retrieved slowly, and for most species near bottom. Large marine worms are surprisingly effective for striped bass, weakfish, and most of the top game fish of inshore and bay waters.

Saltwater Baits

In the vast expanses of saltwater there are three main habitats: the open offshore waters; the surf and near-beach waters; the inside waters of bays and channels. Of the countless varieties of fish life, some are called pelagic, or open-ocean, species, others dwell and feed mostly on bottom either in deep or shallow waters, and many of the most abundant and popular game species roam the inside or bay waters most of their lives. Forage of course differs in these varying habitats. Just like freshwater fish, some marine species have wide-spectrum appetites, while others consume a less varied diet. The chart below does not list everything each species may eat, but it does note baits that are considered standard and most productive for each variety.

Sharks	whole fish, cut bait.
Swordfish	differs from area to area; mackerel, squid among the favorites.
Marlin (all species)	flying fish, mackerel, mullet, bonito, squid, menhaden, small dolphin — whole fish or cut strips.
Sailfish	strip baits from balao, bonito, others; whole mullet or other similar baitfish.
Tuna	herring, mackerel, various baitfish, squid.
Albacore	anchovies, flying fish, various small, lively baitfish.
Bonito	small baitfish, strip baits.
King Mackerel (Kingfish)	strip baits, live shrimp.
Spanish Mackerel	minnows.
Mackerels (various)	minnows, shrimp, small crabs, cut bait.
Wahoo	whole mullet, strip bait, various available baitfishes.
Cobia (Ling)	live shrimp, live crabs, various small baitfish, occasionally cut bait.
Amberjack	strip bait, live mullet, other comparable baitfish.
Pacific Yellowtail	live anchovies, sardines.
Jack Crevalle	live baitfish, cut bait.
Blue Runner	same as above.
Common Pompano	small crustaceans, such as sand fleas, shrimp alive or dead productive on Texas coast.

Permit	hermit crabs, live shrimp.
Bluefish	live shrimp, soft-shelled crabs, eels, menhaden, strip and cut bait.
Dolphin	flying fish, other baitfishes, mullet and other strips.
Tarpon	live shrimp, crabs, pinfish, strip bait.
Bonefish	sand fleas, other crustaceans, hermit crabs, shrimp.
Ladyfish	shrimp, squid, crabs, small fish.
Striped Bass	shrimp, crabs, mullet, other baitfish, clams, bloodworms, cut bait, eels.
Snook	live shrimp, small mullet, crabs.
Great Barracuda	live forage fish, strip baits such as mullet.
Pacific Barracuda	live anchovies, minnows, squid.
Channel Bass (Redfish)	shrimp, alive or peeled, sea worms, crabs, small live mullet, cut bait.
Weakfish (all species)	live shrimp, crabs, sea worms, small fish.
California White Sea Bass	sardines, anchovies, crabs, squid.
Croakers (Atlantic and Pacific)	sea worms, mollusks, crabs, shrimp, cut bait.
California Corbina	live crabs, mollusk meat, pile worms.
Black Drum	cut bait, shrimp, squid, mollusk meat, crabs.
Whiting	cut bait, live or dead shrimp, marine worms.
Snappers (various)	cut bait, shrimp, crabs.
Tautog (Blackfish)	fiddler and green crabs, almost any available bait.
Sheepshead	fiddler crabs, shrimp.
Groupers (various)	cut and strip baits, shrimp, crabs, baitfish.
Jewfish (all varieties)	whole sheepshead or comparable fish, several crabs.
California Black Sea Bass	as above.
Black Sea Bass (Atlantic and Gulf)	shrimp, crabs, skimmer clams, bloodworms.
California Kelp, Sand, Spotted Basses	small live fish, cut bait—almost any bait available.
Tripletail	shrimp, crabs, cut bait.
California Rockfishes (all varieties)	cut bait, chunks of crab or clam, live baitfish.
Cabezon (Pacific)	mussels, sea worms, crabs, cut bait.
Lingcod (Pacific)	cut sardines, shrimp, crabs, squid.
Greenling (Pacific "Seatrout")	cut bait, marine worms, chunks of clam.
Surf perch (all varieties)	any natural Pacific shoreline food available.
Porgies and Grunts	cut bait, any standard regional bait available.
Spadefish	small bits of shrimp or fish.
Codfish	clams, squid, cut bait, live smelt or other small fish.
Pollock	cut bait, clams, squid, small fish.
Halibut, Flounders, other Flatfish	marine worms, shrimp, cut bait, clams, crabs, small baitfish.
Gaff-Topsail Catfish	cut bait, shrimp, crabs.

Index

Aberdeen hook, 9–10
Albacore, bait for, 115, 158
Amberjack, bait for, 158
Anchovies, 115–116, 127, 158, 159
Angleworms, 58–59, 60, 82
Artificial lures, versus bait, 1–5

Bait fishermen versus purists, 1–5
Bait Holder hook, 16, 44, 151–152
Baitfish, freshwater, *see* Minnows
Baitfish, saltwater, 109, 112–123, 158, 159
  anchovies, 115–116, 127, 158, 159
  balao, 119, 129
  butterfish, 119–120
  as chum, 124
  coloring of, 112
  flying fish, 117, 158, 159
  frozen, 113
  killfish, 115
  live, 113
  mackerel, 118, 126, 129
  menhaden, 114, 158
  mullet, 114–115, 126, 129, 158, 159
  needlefish, 117
  oily flesh of, 113
  pinfish, 120
  ribbonfish, 118–119, 123, 124, 128–129
  rigs for, 121–123
  sardines, 116, 126, 127, 158
  silver perch, 119
  silversides, 117
  smelts, 121, 159
Baits, *see* Freshwater baits; Saltwater baits

Balao, 119, 129
Bank sinker, 22, 55, 56
Barnacles, 138
Barracuda, bait for, 116, 129, 130, 159
Bass, bait for, 61, 64–65, 74, 77, 78, 81–85, 87–91, 93, 97, 98, 100, 105
Bates, Joe, 53
Beetles, 104
Bivalve mollusks, 149–153, 158, 159
Black bass, bait for, 64–65, 81, 83
Black drum, bait for, 154, 159
Black sea bass, bait for, 159
Bloodworms, 156, 159
Blue crabs, 144–145
Blue runners, bait for, 158
Bluefish, bait for, 114, 116, 129, 136, 143
Bluegills, bait for, 78, 80, 93, 94, 105, 159
Bobbers, *see* Floats
Bonefish, bait for, 143
Bonito:
  as bait, 129
  bait for, 158, 159
Braided-wire leaders, 30
Bronze finish hooks, 9
Burnham brothers, 77
Butterfish, 119–120

Cabezon, bait for, 143, 159
Cadmium plated hooks, 9
Carlisle hook, 10
Carp:
  as bait, 60–61
  bait for, 106

Casting:
  crayfish, 89–90
  eels, 136
  floats, 26–27
  frogs, 84–86
  grasshoppers, 91
  minnows, 65–67
  night crawlers, 82–83
  saltwater baitfish, 122
  shrimp, 139
  sinkers, 20, 21, 22
  sucker minnows, 73
Casting bubble, 27, 37–38, 50
Catalpa worms, 94
Caterpillars, 60, 94–95
Catfish, bait for, 61, 77, 85–86, 106
Channel bass, bait for, 115, 141, 143, 159
Chubs, bait for, 151
Chumming, 123–126
Chunk-cut baits, 126–128, 159
Ciscoes, bait for, 77, 106
Clams, 124, 149, 150, 151, 152, 159
Clamworms, 156
Clinch sinker, 19–20, 37, 139
Cobia, bait for, 158
Cockroaches, 104
Codfish, bait for, 154, 159
Colorado spinners, 30, 46
Conches, 149, 150
Corbina, bait for, 143, 159
Cork floats, 25, 26, 49
Crabs, 109, 110, 142–146, 158, 159
Crappie, bait for, 60, 62–63, 74, 81, 88
Crayfish, 86–90, 105, 106
Crickets, 18, 90, 91, 93, 105
Croakers, bait for, 109, 143, 159
Crustaceans, saltwater, 109–110, 138–148, 158, 159
  crabs, 109, 110, 142–146, 158, 159
  sand fleas, 109, 110, 146–148, 158, 159
  shrimp, 110, 124, 138–142, 158, 159
Cut bait:
  freshwater, 74–77, 105, 106
  saltwater, 116, 117, 118, 126–135, 158, 159

Dipsey sinker, 20–21, 39, 42, 55, 56, 65
Dodgers, 30
Dolphins, bait for, 119, 129, 134, 159
Double bait hooks, 12–13
Downrigger trolling device, 22, 46–47

Dragonflies, 104
Drail, 24
Drum (freshwater), bait for, 77, 88, 106
Drum (saltwater), bait for, 109, 154, 159

Eagle Claw hooks, 11, 16, 44
Eels, 135–137, 159
Egg sinker, 21, 42, 44

Fiddler crabs, 109, 110, 124, 143, 159
Fish-finder rig:
  freshwater, 32, 42–44, 82
  saltwater, 51–53
Flashers, 30
Flatfishes, bait for, 143, 159
Floats, 24–28
  casting bubble, 27, 37–38, 50
  in freshwater rigs, 34–38
  popping-cork, 26, 49–50, 139
  in saltwater rigs, 48–52
Flounder, bait for, 154, 159
Flying fish, 117, 158, 159
Free-line rig, see Fish-finder rig
Freshwater baits:
  caterpillars, 60, 94–95
  choosing, 58–60
  crayfish, 86–90, 105, 106
  crickets, 18, 90, 91, 93, 105
  cut, 74–77, 105, 106
  flying insects, 60, 104–105, 106
  freshwater mussels, 103
  frogs, 83–86, 105
  grasshoppers, 90–93, 105
  grubs, 60, 94–95
  hellgrammites, 95–97
  leeches, 104–105, 106
  minnows, see Minnows
  natural bait, defined, 58
  night crawlers, see Night crawlers
  nymphs, 60, 95–97, 105, 106
  salamanders, 97–100, 105, 106
  salmon eggs, 16, 43–45, 101–103, 106
  worms, 58–59, 60, 77–83, 105, 106, 110
Freshwater rigs, 33–47
  with bait only, 38–39
  cut bait and, 74–75
  downrigger trolling device, 46–47
  fish-finder, 32, 42–44, 82
  with floats, 34–38
  for minnow fishing, 65–70
  for salmon egg fishing, 43–45, 101–102
  sinker-on-end-of-line, 39–41, 82

with sinkers only, 39–47
with spinners, 45, 46
split shot in, 33–34
for sucker minnow fishing, 71–73
worm harness, 45–46, 79
See also freshwater baits; Hooking
Frog harness, 15
Frogs, 83–86, 105

Ghost crabs, 143
Ghost shrimp, 138–139
Gizzard shad, 77
Gold finish hooks, 9
Grass shrimp, 140–141
Grasshoppers, 90–93, 105
Green crabs, 159
Greenline, bait for, 159
Groupers, bait for, 129, 143, 159
Grubs, 60, 94–95
Grunts, bait for, 121, 151, 159

Hellgrammites, 95–97
Hermit crabs, 144, 159
Hi-Lo Rig, 55
Hooking:
    anchovies, 116
    caterpillars, 94, 95
    crayfish, 87–90
    cut bait, 127–128, 131–135
    eels, 136
    frogs, 84
    grasshoppers, 91–93
    grubs, 95
    hellgrammites, 96
    marine worms, 157–158
    minnows, 66–69, 71
    mollusks, 149, 151–154
    night crawlers, 79–80, 81–82
    salamanders, 97, 98, 100
    salmon eggs, 101–102
    saltwater baitfish, 122, 123
    sand fleas, 147, 148
    sardines, 116
    shrimp, 139–142
    squid, 154–155
    sucker minnows, 71
    worms, 78–79
Hooks, 8–17
    attaching bait to, *see* Hooking
    bait-holder, 16, 44, 151–152
    double, 12–13
    early, 8

finishes, 9
fish species and, 91
frog harness, 15
for ice fishing, 12
for minnow fishing, 10, 12–14
for night-crawler fishing, 10, 16
point styles, 16–17
popular designs, 9–11
safety pin, 13
for salmon-eggs, 16, 44, 101
shank size, 16
sizes, 17
treble, 15–16, 50, 70, 139–140
weedless, 11–12
wide-gap bend, 11
See also Freshwater rigs; Saltwater
    rigs

Indiana spinners, 30
Insects, flying, 60, 104–105, 106

Jack crevalle, bait for, 158
Jewfish, bait for, 159
June-bug spinner, 30, 46

Kahle horizontal hook, 12
Keel sinker, 22
Killfish, 115
King mackerel (Kingfish), bait for, 119,
    129, 158
Kirby hook, 10–11

Ladyfish, bait for, 159
Lead shot, split, 18
Lead strips, wrap-on, 19
Leaders, 29–30, 44, 56
Leaf sinker, 23
Leeches, 104–105, 106
Limerick hook, 11
Line, 29–30, 36
Lingcod, bait for, 143, 154, 159
Lobsters, 138

Mackerel:
    as bait, 118, 126, 129
    bait for, 116, 158
Marine worms, 110, 155–159
Marlin, bait for, 129, 134, 154, 158
Menhaden, 114, 158
Minnows, 60–71, 158, 159
    casting, 65–67
    dead, 63, 66–69
    defined, 60–61

Minnows (*Continued*)
   diet of game fish and, 61–65
   hooking, 66–69, 71
   hooks for, 10, 12–14
   live, 64, 65–66, 71–73
   obtaining, 71
   rigs for fishing, 65–70
   sinkers for, 17, 18
   stream fishing, 71
   sucker, 61, 71–75
   trolling, 67–68, 69
Model Perfect hook, 11
Mollusks, 103, 105, 106, 109, 110, 149–155
   bivalve and univalve, 149–153, 158, 159
   squid, 110, 153–155, 158, 159
Monofil lines, 29–30, 36
Mooching, 132–133
Mud-puppy, 110
Mullet, 114–115, 126, 158, 159
Muskellange, bait for, 60, 71–74, 105
Mussels:
   fresh water, 103
   saltwater, 149, 152

Needlefish, 117
Newts, 97, 98
Night crawlers, 59, 60, 78–83, 105, 106
   casting, 82–83
   hooking, 79–80, 81–82
   hooks for, 10, 16
   sinkers for, 21
   worm harness for, 45–46, 79
Nymphs, 60, 95–97, 105, 106

O'Shaughnessy hook, 11, 17
Oysters, 150, 151

Pencil lead, 44–45
Perch, bait for, 59, 61, 63, 64, 74, 77, 81, 87, 93, 105
Permit, bait for, 159
Piano-wire leaders, 30
Pickerel, bait for, 65, 74, 105
Pike, bait for, 60, 61, 65, 74, 85, 105
Pinfish, 120
Plastic beads, 36–37
Plastic floats, 25
Plug cut, 132–133
Pollock, bait for, 154
Pompano, bait for, 147–148, 158
Popping-cork floats, 26, 49–50, 139

Porgies, bait for, 159
Pyramid sinker, 23, 52, 56

Quill floats, 27–28

Redfish, *see* Channel bass
Ribbonfish, 118–119, 123, 124, 128–129
Rigs, 32–57
   defined, 32
   See also Freshwater rigs; Saltwater rigs
Rock bass, bait for, 93, 105
Rock crabs, 144
Rockfish, bait for, 139, 159
Roe, *see* Salmon eggs

Sacramento perch, bait for, 105
Safety-pin hooks, 13
Sailfish, bait for, 134, 158
Salamanders, 97–100, 105, 106
Salmon, mooching for, 132–133
Salmon eggs, 16, 43–45, 101–103, 106
Saltwater baits, 2, 107–159
   baitfish, *see* Baitfish, saltwater
   crustaceans, *see* Crustaceans, saltwater
   cut bait, 116, 117, 118, 126–135, 158, 159
   chumming, 123–126
   eels, 135–137, 159
   game species and, 107–109
   hooks for, 16
   marine worms, 110, 155–159
   mollusks, *see* Mollusks
   water motion and, 111
Saltwater rigs, 47–57, 110, 121–123
   with bait only, 53–54
   fish-finder, 51–53
   with floats, 48–52
   sinker-on-end-of-line, 54–57, 122
   See also Freshwater rigs
Sand fleas, 109, 110, 146–148, 158, 159
Sand lance, 137
Sardines, 116, 126, 127, 158
Sea catfish, 121
Sharks, bait for, 114, 119, 123, 158
Sheepshead, bait for, 109, 143, 159
Shore crabs, 144
Shrimp, 15–16, 110, 124, 138–142, 158, 159
Silver perch, 119
Silversides, 117
Sinkers, 17–24
   bank, 22, 55, 56
   casting, 20, 21, 22

clinch, 19–20, 37, 139
dipsey, 20–21, 39, 42, 55, 56, 65
drail, 24
in egg cluster fishing rigs, 44–45
on end of line, 39–41, 54–57, 82, 122
finishes, 24
in fish-finder rigs, 42–44, 51–53
in freshwater rigs, 33–47
pencil leads, 44–45
pyramid, 23, 52, 56
in rigs with floats, 34–38, 48–52
in saltwater rigs, 48–57
sizes, 17
slip, 21, 32, 42–44, 82
snagless, 23, 42
split shot, 18, 33–34, 43, 66, 82
trolling, 21, 22, 46–47, 50, 69–70
walking, 24, 42
wrap-on lead strips, 19
See also Freshwater rigs; Saltwater rigs
Siren, 100
Slip sinkers, 21, 32, 42–44, 82
Smelts, 121, 159
Snagless sinker, 23, 42
Snappers, bait for, 126, 151, 154, 158, 159
Snaps, 28–29, 56–57
Snook, bait for, 159
Spadefish, bait for, 128, 159
Spanish mackerel, bait for, 158
Speckled trout, *see* Weakfish, bait for
Spinners, 30, 45, 46
Split shot, 18, 33–34, 43, 66, 82
Spreader, 42, 56
Sproat hook, 11
Squid, 110, 153–155, 158, 159
Stainless-steel hooks, 9
Stop-knot, 36–37
Streever, Fred, 14
Strip bait, 128–135, 158–159
Striped anchovy, 116
Striped bass, bait for, 114, 116, 136, 140, 143, 154, 159
Sucker minnows, 61, 71–75
Sunfish:
  as bait, 61
  bait for, 60–62, 74, 78, 88, 91, 93, 97, 103, 105
Surfperch, bait for, 159
Swivels, 22, 28–29, 39, 43, 45, 51, 56–57
Swordfish, bait for, 154, 158

Tadpoles, 86
Tarpon, bait for, 120, 143, 159
Tautog, bait for, 109, 143, 159
Texas rig, 80
Three-way swivel, 29, 39, 45, 51, 56–57
Throat latch, 76–77
Tin-plated hooks, 9
Toads, 86
Treble hooks, 15–16, 50, 70, 139–140
Tripletail, bait for, 159
Trolling:
  downrigger device for, 22, 46–47
  eels, 136
  minnows, 67–68, 69
  sinkers, 21, 22, 46–47, 50, 69–70
  squid, 154–155
  strip bait, 128, 132
Trout, bait for, 61, 75–76, 78, 83, 91, 93, 97–98, 100, 101, 106
Tube worms, 156–157
Tunas, bait for, 114, 116, 119, 154, 158

Wahoo, bait for, 129, 158
Walking sinker, 24, 42
Walleye, bait for, 59, 61, 63–64, 71, 80–81, 105
Walton, Izaak, 3
Warmouths, bait for, 78, 105
Waterdogs, *see* Salamanders
Waxworms, 94
Weakfish, bait for, 125, 139, 140, 143, 159
Weedless hooks, 11–12
Whelks, 150
White bass, bait for, 64, 76, 93
White perch, bait for, 64, 77, 105
White sea bass, bait for, 154, 159
Whitefish, bait for, 77, 106
Whiting, bait for, 159
Wigglers, 97
Worm harness, 45–46, 79
Worms, 77–83, 97, 105, 106, 110
  angleworms, 58–59, 60, 82
  marine, 110, 155–159
  See also Night crawlers
Wrap-on lead strips, 19

Yellow bass, bait for, 64, 77
Yellow perch, bait for, 63, 74, 81, 87, 93
Young, Paul, 53